T0207979

SOS: SIMPLICITY OF SOUL

THE SECRET OF LIVING THROUGH YOUR SOUL

KATHLEEN ANN PICKERING

BALBOA.PRESS

A DIVISION OF HAY HOUSE

Balboa Press books may be ordered through booksellers or by contacting:

Balboa Press
A Division of Hay House
1663 Liberty Drive
Bloomington, IN 47403
www.balboapress.com
844-682-1282

Because of the dynamic nature of the Internet, any web addresses or
links contained in this book may have changed since publication and
may no longer be valid. The views expressed in this work are solely those
of the author and do not necessarily reflect the views of the publisher,
and the publisher hereby disclaims any responsibility for them.

The author of this book does not dispense medical advice or prescribe the use
of any technique as a form of treatment for physical, emotional, or medical
problems without the advice of a physician, either directly or indirectly. The
intent of the author is only to offer information of a general nature to help
you in your quest for emotional and spiritual well-being. In the event you use
any of the information in this book for yourself, which is your constitutional
right, the author and the publisher assume no responsibility for your actions.

Any people depicted in stock imagery provided by Getty Images are
models, and such images are being used for illustrative purposes only.
Certain stock imagery © Getty Images.

Print information available on the last page.

ISBN: 978-1-9822-3975-6 (sc)
ISBN: 978-1-9822-3976-3 (e)

Balboa Press rev. date: 11/10/2022

CONTENTS

This book is dedicated to you.

AUTHOR'S NOTE

This book:

- Presents this author's recollection of an unbelievable, yet true, encounter with a Being of Love, Energy and Light—the Holy Spirit.

- Shares the turbulent, exciting, and insightful effect the message from this extraordinary encounter had on this author while she grappled with the information through the years.

- Explains the results of finally understanding the profound message from this Being, who had only one intention: To reveal the enormous power of God's love as a creative tool available to us through our souls.

- Is an invitation to adjust your world view to incorporate a dimension of existence that for most living beings goes untapped. This untapped resource, the soul, exists within us to fuel all our talents, enrich our presence, and fulfill our life's purpose, now!

- Challenges you to seek your joy as intended through the power of Creation and make an impact in the world by achieving personal success for your happiness and the happiness of generations to come. This is SOS: Simplicity of Soul.

CHAPTER ONE

Who Are We and Why Are We Here?

Who has the audacity to claim they know who we are and why we are here? With the greatest humility, I claim, I do.

I wrote Simplicity of Soul for you. SOS is my invitation for you to fully understand the singular and exquisite purpose of our Existence: To participate in the evolution of Creation simply by being our unique selves.

Do you and I really have a role in Creation? Could the meaning of our existence be so simple? The answer to both questions is yes. If you will allow me, I shall share what I have learned about our role in Creation, and how it applies to you on your life's journey.

I invite you to consider a power greater than we, who from sheer love, endowed us with the twin gifts of a Soul, as a continued connection to Creation, and Free Will, to determine as individuals the use of our faculties, our environment, and our bodies for our highest good. SOS is a book about spiritual awakening and understanding. I have no intention of touting religion, but to share a fundament truth that I have learned. I will show you how the soul, when used as the core motivator to achieve your desired goals and personal joy, continues the purpose of life to your benefit and the benefit of all.

Clearly, in today's world there is a clamoring for more meaning in our lives. The media teems with spiritual growth gurus offering insights to personal wholeness. Everywhere we hear concern for the deterioration of tradition, personal freedoms, economic conditions, and the future to be inherited by generations to come. Throughout the ages, these concerns have been a driving force in one form or another behind humanity's evolution—but never more than now.

By the grace of God, I had an experience that opened my eyes to the Truth. This experience transformed my understanding of life and my unique role in the world.

I understand the responsibility and power humanity holds to create abundant, joyful lives, individually and beneficially for each other and the planet. I am hoping to do the same for you.

I'm sure many of us, in sound mind and body, can relate a time when we experienced a surreal event, knew it happened, but could not prove it. Does lack of proof make that experience unreal? If you are of sound mind and body? No. It means we do not have enough knowledge to explain the phenomena.

The information I am sharing in this book holds little proof, except life experiences and the results thereof. It will take a leap of faith on your part, as it did for me, because the blatant truth, no matter how challenging, is hard to ignore. I offer my word, and my unwavering belief, that my extraordinary encounter was indeed real and launched all the possibilities I present here. I could be mistaken, but with every fiber of my being, I suspect not. I ask you to explore the possibilities I offer and use your own judgement. You may disagree, or you may awaken something you have always known but had not recognized, until now.

So, my significant, life changing event is:

I stood face-to-face with the Holy Spirit.

There, I said it. I know there are others who make the same claim, because they have told me of similar experiences, perhaps not what I visually encountered, but soulfully expressed their unique experience with the same results. Like me, their lives were changed for good, forever.

More importantly, there are those of you who are giving this page a sidelong glance and questioning the likelihood of such an encounter. No worries. My initial response to such skepticism is why I delayed years before deciding to share this incredible news.

My experience was so significant and life-altering, that in a perfect world, sharing this event should have been effortless all those years ago. I was wrong.

The truth of the matter is, my new insights so diametrically oppose today's life structure, that people shied away from me. Most folks thought I'd become unhinged. And rightfully so! The entire event sounded unbelievable. I could not prove what I had experienced in a world which requires proof. So, I stopped talking. More importantly, I needed time to get my emotions in check to fully understand what had happened.

Now, I can share with a calmer heart. I want to show you what the Holy Spirit shared with me as the exquisite intention behind Creation—including you and me. I want to explain how easy and soulful our approach to life can be—no matter how wonderful or turbulent the circumstances. I want you to understand that you and I are not alone in this world. We are not random. We are an intended and purposeful outpouring of the ever-changing tapestry of Creation.

And why were we born? So that the miracle of Creation can continue flowing through us. Each of us is still connected to our Source. Each of us is intended to thrive through soul-driven love, bringing our unique talents, no matter how great or small, into the world as an extension of God working through us, and us through Him.

Mind boggling.

The fact that I learned this information from the Holy Spirit in a moment of panic still amazes me. But I did. I believe the catalyst behind this profound information, already carried within us, is the answer to what ails humanity. I know. Huge claim. Please give me a little more of your time so I may explain further.

First, what events created the fertile ground for my encounter?

I suspect that I experienced this gift of the Holy Spirit as a twenty-three-year-old, because since I was a child, I'd been searching for answers to 'Who am I?

5

Why am I here?' From an early age, my emphatically Catholic mother taught me and my siblings about God, heaven, and prayer. I dare say, I was fascinated. I loved the concept of a spiritual God, and constantly asked Him why I was here. (I was a weird kid.) Why I wanted to know at such a young age, I still don't understand. But, in the end, I think my belief in God and my continued desire to know Him brought me the answer, through my soul, as an adult when I could appreciate and act on the information.

My initial challenge after experiencing this event: Telling my story without sounding crazy. Unfortunately, I delivered the information incorrectly—with tears and trembling. My experience had been so overwhelming, that quite frankly, I don't think I would have believed me! Constant skepticism, and well-meant advice from friends and family members, finally silenced me. I never questioned what I had seen and learned but felt awful that my story distressed others.

The gift of time has been a blessing. I am stronger and more aware of the true nature of my experience. Today, I understand the full power behind the information. And the best part? I believe you will love it.

Here are my thoughts and my story:

As each of us does, I experienced moments in life, which for better or worse, formed my world view. Mine were rather colorful moments, both good and bad. No need to explore them in depth at this point but sharing a bit about me will help explain my motive behind this book.

This may sound odd, or you may feel the same, but from a very young age, I was aware of an intrinsic nature residing within me, as if there was more to me than my body. I also recognized the sensitivities of my emotional mother, the distinct differences among my siblings, and my rough-and-tumble father who loved to laugh. I wanted to make sure everyone around me was happy, especially because by the age of four, I realized my mother was not.

Born the second oldest of eight children into an Irish-Catholic/German-Protestant family, this cultural mix made for an interesting blend of strong work ethic coupled with a deep-seated fear for the wrath of God. As a child, I was taught I possessed a soul, which confirmed my awareness of the unrecognizable nature within me. I was also taught I had to first, protect my soul from evil—a lesson I honor, and second, that God could strike with punishment at any given moment if I did something wrong. On point two, I have learned differently, which I will explain further on.

Again, while this book is not a discourse on any religion, I speak about a Catholic background because it helps pave my track leading to the present moment. Please indulge me on this one point.

My parochial grammar school presented the personalities in the Old and New Testament, as if all were part of my family tree. Most of those stories either frightened me, sparked my compassion, or confused the hell out of me; but every story was riveting. I loved the more modern stories about Mary, the mother of Jesus, appearing to young children in Fatima, Lourdes, Guadalupe, and now, present day in Medjugorje. As a young girl, I used to whisper prayers at night in my bunk bed and beg the Blessed Mother to appear to me. Why not? I was a good kid. Besides, I wanted to meet her, too. As you can imagine, I heard nothing. Not a peep.

Yet, from the beginning, my religion demanded I accept unexplainable dogma through faith. Faith, defined as *complete trust in something for which there is no proof,* made it much easier to accept the unexplainable events happening in life. To this day, I claim this one unusual experience helped me understand the Truth through my willingness to believe the unbelievable. This willingness came from Faith. And Faith has brought results.

First, let me tell you what I know to be the Truth, and then I'll explain how I arrived at this conclusion.

The Truth: Creation manifested as an explosion of conscious, exquisite, and unbridled love. Through our souls, you and I exist as conduits to continue this outpouring of love. How? Through living, breathing, experiencing, and creating more love—love of others, love of our chosen talents and careers, love of nature and the earth, love of ourselves as creations of God—all by simply by being who we were born to be. The soul is the tool, the catalyst, and the real missing secret behind understanding our existence. I call this understanding, SOS: Simplicity of Soul. This Truth, when fully understood, will bring your life, and the world, back into the immutable, living current of creation of which we are an inextricable part.

If this statement raises doubt, I ask you to consider science and the amazing understanding we now have of the interrelation between animals, nature, and the planet. Consider the alarming effects generations of humans are having on the planet because of the blindness to the roles we play outside the natural course of Creation. Creation is not past tense. Creation continues now as you read this. If we truly understood that within us, we possess the tools to be intrinsic, positive players in Creation, our vision would clear.

Each of us possesses tools of Creation within our nature. While we are aware of some of these tools, i.e., intelligence and ego, the most powerful and most pure of these tools is our soul. In this dialogue, my primary focus is to show the reality and purpose of our souls as a tool for use, now. I am inviting you to awaken and tap into the power of your soul. By telling you the story behind my soul's awakening, I believe your soul will hear me.

Here are the facts behind Simplicity of Soul:

1. Every molecule of Creation, including you, me, and everywhere we can and cannot see, is an integral and much cherished element encompassing one huge body of Existence. There is absolutely no disconnection anywhere.

2. You and I are not solitary beings, apart from the world around us. Singly, we are a unique and important thread woven into the intricate tapestry of life, contributing, experiencing, and sensing the world around us as the single body of Existence.

3. In addition, this physical body of existence (God) created us as an integral part of itself (Himself) to pursue love and creation through us. For us, intelligence is fueled through learning; ego is

SOS: Simplicity Of Soul

fueled through accomplishment; and the soul conveys God's love through our entire creative process.

What many of us miss as fact is that the non-physical essences of intelligence and ego may become flawed or unformed within us from life experience, while our soul is constant and absolute perfection and balances our intelligence and ego. Only when ego, intelligence, and soul function equally, like a unilateral triangle, can all our talents blend perfectly with existence.

What I love most about this Truth is the fact that if our soul is perfect, then, so are we. I know. This statement contradicts the popular belief of an imperfect humanity in an imperfect world. The world (Creation) is perfect. Humanity's lack of soul-driven behavior throughout the ages has created the proverbial imperfect world. Humanity is an amazing creation, born perfectly to reflect the perfection from which we were created. Yet, we fail to see this. Our clarity is clouded with over-active ego behavior that drives the intellect in wrong directions.

Now, you may jump to thinking that birth defects, deformities of mind and body from life experiences, and untimely deaths are not perfection, but those points return full circle to the truth of the soul's value when soul thinking is fully understood. I am hoping to illuminate this fact as we continue.

What is the soul? Merriam Webster Dictionary defines soul as *the immaterial essence, animating principle, or actuating cause of an individual life; the spiritual principle embodied in human beings, all rational or spiritual beings, or the universe.*

The Cambridge English Dictionary describes the soul as *the spiritual part of a person that some people believe continues to exist in some form after their body has died—or the part of a person that is not physical and experiences deep feelings and emotions.*

Ancient Egyptians believed the soul had five parts: a name, a shadow, a heart, personality, and vital fire. The Hebrew word for soul is *Nefesh*. And in the Bible, Isaiah 58:10–12 says this about the soul: *"If you extend your soul to the hungry, and satisfy the afflicted, then your light shall dawn in the darkness, and your darkness shall be as the noonday. The Lord will guide you continually, and satisfy your soul in drought, strengthen your bones; and you shall be like a watered garden, and like a spring of water, whose waters do not fail. And the places that have been desolate for ages shall be built in thee: thou shalt raise up the foundations of generation and generation: and thou shalt be called the repairer of the fences, turning the paths into rest."*

These are four examples, but with more research almost every culture and/or religion describes the soul in one form or another. Knowing this, I fail to understand why humanity has not fully acknowledged the soul its rightful place in the business of life!

Through the soul, the truth of our perfection defies our imperfections, because through our imperfections we reach Truth. What was repeatedly taught to me as divine punishment for sins, opposes what I learned from the Holy Spirit about God and Existence. All religions branch from the core belief of a power greater than we, fueled by a deep and abiding love for all Creation. Yet perhaps many religions interpreted their foundations on humanity's unworthiness instead of the fact that we are worthy creations of love. This mistake is critical.

Inhabitants of this earth who espouse we are flawed, and imperfect, will never understand the true purpose of their own birth. We are, in fact, a perfect creation, flaws and all. We were created by intense love and intended to continue creating love through our soul connection to our Creator. We may be born with birth defects, or accumulate flaws through life experiences, but by loving ourselves and each other, flaws and all, the perfection of Creation continues. And what is beautiful, is that should this belief in our perfection as a creation of God grow humbly stronger within us, and be understood by future generations, imperfections and flaws will eventually cease. Life on earth could be as Jesus taught in The Lord's Prayer: "...*Thy will be done on earth as it is in Heaven.*"

God exists. Our tie to God through our souls is what creates our spirituality. Our souls do not make us gods; our souls make us extensions of God's creation. This is how we serve God and each other—and vice versa.

It took me forty years to drum up the nerve to write about my experience without offering proof. While I know I encountered the Holy Spirit, he did not introduce himself as such. My soul, however, tells me this intense, overwhelmingly loving Presence was, indeed, the Holy Spirit. Simply stated, He knew me, and I recognized Him as the Creator of Life.

Honestly, as the years progressed, I had times where the ground was fertile for soulful discussion with others, so I took the chance. To my delight, I received encouragement, conversation after conversation, coincidence after coincidence to make me realize I should share my encounter. Especially now. Our planet cannot handle too many more of our mistakes. And worse, our souls cannot withstand much more of the abuse we heap upon our bodies from the lack of love we hold for ourselves. Therefore, I chose the acronym,

SOS for Simplicity of Soul. SOS is the international signal for help.

I have answers. And I hope these answers bring insight. I will list these surprisingly safe answers very shortly. Please note, I use the word safe with purpose, because wanting to feel safe is the driving force behind choices we make.

But first, I'd like to explain the encounter I experienced and work our way from there. It will help you understand how I arrived at these conclusions. Please, read on.

CHAPTER TWO

Understanding the Truth

The year was 1979. At twenty-three, I was a newlywed and preparing to relocate from my New York home to Florida where my husband had taken a job.

Our planned move distressed my mother. Up to this point, none of her eight children had left home, except me. I attended college in Arizona five years earlier, which to my surprise, caused all sorts of strife on the home front. Mom and Dad didn't like when anyone strayed far from the family circle. They thought my need to test my independence at college was a good idea at the time, but once I was gone, changed their minds.

Despite their conclusions, moving to Arizona proved beneficial for me. As all risks taken, the adventure to the Sonoran Desert set the course of my life into motion, which included returning to New York with the man I eventually married.

So, my new husband and I were scheduled to move away in a week. My mother said she wanted to take a road trip together as a getaway before we left town. I said, "Sure! Where do you want to go?"

She said, "It's a surprise."

Early the next morning, my youngest sister, two younger brothers and I climbed into Mom's sleek, brown Cadillac and took off north on Interstate 95. Now, I don't know about you, but to me, a surprise road trip would be to a destination such as a spa, a beautiful beach, a state park, a country fair, splurge shopping at some decadent store. Something fun, no?

Imagine my surprise, and the surprise of my siblings, when Mother pulled into the parking lot of an outdated but charming Catholic church in Worcester, Massachusetts. Please, don't get me wrong. I find no fault with charming churches. This stop simply was not my idea of a surprise road trip.

So, when Mother announced we were attending a charismatic healing service, I wanted to jump out of my skin. A healing service? Did I need healing? No wonder she didn't reveal our destination. None of us would have gotten into the car. Surprise, indeed!

Since a healing service attracts some of the most trusting, needy, and frightened folks seeking help (such as my mother), I became defensive. I decided, right then and there, if I detected any duplicity on the part of this priest for whom Mother had driven hours to see, I would stand up and challenge him for taking advantage of people willing to trust in him as an agent of love, truth, and God.

Without a chance to cement my resolve, Mother herded us into the packed-to-the-rafters church only to find standing room in the balcony surrounding the church gallery below. I could see almost nothing except the crush of folks in front of us, and everyone was talking with excitement.

I immediately became aware of amazing, ethereal music penetrating my hearing. If I were to imagine angels singing, I'd swear these hymns were theirs. This music became the only sound I could hear. I'd never heard such perfect voices ever before, or since. I sat on a step and began weeping. Why? Not sure. But the tears seemed cleansing, as if I carried sadness, either for the people around me or for my own place in the world. The music was transforming my sadness into peace.

Mine were tears of gratitude and I could not stop. My younger brother questioned me, and I just shrugged and said, "It's the music. I feel so foolish!"

Moments later a man began speaking through a microphone, and the church grew quiet. Standing along the back wall of the balcony I could not see him, but I remember thinking, "I'd bet Christ sounded like this man."

The young, dark-haired man walking up the center isle was Father Ralph DiOrio, a Catholic priest who was quickly making his mark in the religious community as a healer. As a spiritual woman, I was curious to learn about this man. As a woman with reasonable intellect, I didn't quite trust evangelical healing ministries. I believe Jesus Christ performed miracles, but the very real fact that people have scammed innocent believers in the name of God for their own advancement was not lost on me. Yet, the gentleness and the purity in this man's voice captivated my attention. Instinctually, I sensed he was someone special, gifted, holy. No pomp. No circumstance. Humble.

I was ready to be proven wrong. I wanted to hear everything this priest had to say. Now, friends and colleagues who have read this work for me have suggested I leave the following paragraph out, because it raises flags as to the credibility of my story. I know they are correct, but I cannot omit this information. Doing so will protect my credibility but will cheat the reader of the possibility of understanding the depth of what humanity can achieve when soul-connected to God, as was intended in our creation in the first place. So, please stay with me a bit longer and consider the possibilities.

After Father DiOrio explained how the next hour would unfold, I worked my way to the edge of the balcony as assistants starting to bring people forward from the crowd. Father DiOrio prayed over people who trusted and believed they were healed. They'd find out for sure when they went home and visited their doctors. Ok. Everything looked status quo to me. Then, from my bird's eye view, I watched directly below me, as Fr. DiOrio prayed over a boy in a wheelchair. Imagine my shock, as I witnessed the boy's one shorter leg grow to match his other healthy leg. My mind could hardly register what happened. None of the other healings in the church appeared as obvious, since they were internal illnesses, but I know I saw the boy's leg grow. Viewing the sight rattled me right down to my toes.

This is insane, right? These sorts of events don't happen in real life. But . . . what if? In my later research on Fr. DiOrio, I found the Catholic church recognized DiOrio's talent as a healer, but also found him controversial. I found articles quoting him as saying he didn't ask for this gift of healing. The talent simply happened. Early in his priesthood, he discovered when he brought the sacraments to ailing people, they became well. After a while, he stopped resisting and claimed this unbelievable talent as a gift from God. And I, skeptic that I was, saw first-hand, and in fact, he healed people.

Think about it. What if we all trusted the purity and perfection of our Creator? We could create. We could heal as servants of God if healing is our God-given gift. Doesn't the bible cite that on the sixth day of Creation, God created man in his image and likeness? If we are "chips off the old block" as they say about offspring, then we carry God within us as our children carry us in their DNA. We are in our Creator as much as our Creator resides within us. One. Connected. Through our souls. Created to create, rejoice and be glad. This understanding would make Father DiOrio perfectly capable to heal with the power of God through his soul, because healing was his individual calling. This realization, when understood, is humbling and beautiful.

We have souls to continually celebrate God's creation. Souls are our umbilical cord to our Creator. Our souls are our lifeline to Infinity, giving us, through our bodies, the ability to expand God further through our own existence on this amazing, rejuvenating jewel, the Earth.

Once again, I am not saying we are gods, separate from God. I am saying we were created to continue God's creation. Think about it. Trees continue to create oxygen for the air, the oceans continually cleanse and renew, the earth effortlessly sprouts life, and on and on. As children of God our purpose is to use our wondrous intellects to enhance God's world, soulfully. It's like signing up for the most amazing career on Earth: simply by being ourselves, offering the talents with which we were born to continue weaving the tapestry of life.

The Earth could very well be Eden. Biblical Adam and Eve lost Eden due to a newly awakened, ego-generated change within their intellect—described as eating forbidden fruit and suddenly becoming self-conscious. Why? Because once removed from the soul connection to God, a human being senses fear, and fear generates mistrust, at best. The serpent represents egoic thought invading the purity of Eden. Could it be the serpent's (ego's) argument that God kept Adam and Eve from the tree of knowledge because God did not want them to know what He knows gave their awakened egos power over their souls, and thus separated them from the peace of God? If so, this action created the first strife. From there, Adam and Eve mis-understood God's Truth.

Choosing to accept doubt in God made Adam and Eve blind to Eden. I suggest the cherubim described in the bible as guarding Eden to keep them out was the barrier created by Adam and Eve's awakened ego in their sudden understanding of good and evil. Eden was only good (innocence and perfection) while evil had no home in Eden. Adam and Eve suddenly saw themselves as separate from God and the rest of Creation, and in accepting this belief through Free Will, abandoned their perfect existence within Eden and their soul connection to God. More on this topic later.

Back to my story.

After Father DiOrio finished his healings, the congregation dismissed for lunch, to return in an hour. My mother did not want to miss a minute of the next half of the service, so we ate sandwiches from paper lunch bags she had prepared in advance.

Even though I had witnessed Father DiOrio heal the boy in the wheelchair, a healthy dose of disbelief rose after discussing with my siblings what I'd seen from my view on the balcony. Ignoring my mother's irritation, and my inability at the time to understand the true meaning of what I witnessed, my siblings and I decided that unless we saw proof, there had to be a gimmick here. The morning's events simply could not have been possible.

Since it only took twenty minutes to eat, Mom rushed us back into the church to find better seats.

The five of us ended up in wooden pews smack in the middle of the church. I was surprised at how quickly the church filled to the balcony, once again. I expected to hear more amazing music, but no. It wasn't long before Father DiOrio returned. Quiet, peaceful as before, and meditative. If he knew what was about to happen, how did he keep so cool?

Father DiOrio invited everyone to stand and hold hands with the person next to them. He asked us to close our eyes and listen as he prayed out loud. He said our silence and listening made his prayer our own, and therefore more powerful. So, he began.

I cannot remember everything he said. I remember the spoke of the power of angels (which had me wondering if the amazing music I heard earlier had been angels) and the strength of our guardian angels. He honored the beauty of the earth and the breath of the Holy Spirit present on the planet. And then, with my eyes closed, the clatter began. Thump. Bump. Bump. I opened my eyes. All around me people were falling. In front of me. Behind me. Above in the balcony, one man seemed unconscious and was hanging over the railing.

People began shouting. Women screamed. Father DiOrio instructed everyone not to touch anyone who'd fallen. He explained that the Holy Spirit united with their souls and their bodies lost motor skills. They were unharmed. Having a spiritual moment. If we touched them, it would break the connection with the Divine.

Nope. I didn't accept his explanation. Those prone bodies didn't look happy at all. I felt like we were ambushed. Terrified, my younger sister broke her handhold with my brother and bolted from the church. I learned afterwards that she locked herself in the car and cried. None of my family members had "gone down" as I called it, but my mother swayed ominously. As a child, I fainted a lot, and I hated the feeling. Horrified, I jammed my eyes shut and said this prayer as fervently as I could to the one and only God I know.

I said, "God, I know you're out there, and you know I love you. But listen and listen well. I am NOT GOING DOWN!"

At that moment, with my eyes closed, this brilliant, overwhelmingly spotlight-white light ignited inside my head. I felt as if I mentally squinted to shield my eyes from the brightness. When I could no longer bear such intensity, a golden triangle appeared, growing larger inside my head. I calmed, and became mesmerized by the sharp, linear edges shimmering with molten, liquid gold moving as if alive and pulsing within the narrow channel of the triangle. I remember sighing out loud. The sight was exquisite!

Now, I am not kidding when I tell you what happened next. Inside this brilliant and spectacular, gold-blazing triangle, an eye appeared. Long lashed and closed, the eye opened. I can't be sure of the color, but I'd say light blue, like the most perfect sun filled day. Now, as the eye opened, I felt something inside me move. I was lifted on a current of energy, my arms outstretched like flying. I was still standing, holding hands with my mother and brother. Yet, I was in motion, moving from within my body and streaming towards and through the eye's pupil, like sailing through a porthole into the Universe.

It wasn't until later I realized my soul had connected with this power while my body stood still. I could see where I was traveling, which proved to me my soul has vision. I was intact. Whole, yet without my body. I was consciously experiencing my soul, freed from the physical. We have all heard of near-death experiences where a person leaves their body and observes all around them. This was similar, except I streamed into the universe with nothing before me but stars, galaxies, and unending Ether.

Can you imagine this story coming from a good Catholic, raised by the rules, don't-question-only-obey-type of girl? Insane, I know! But, let me continue because my story gets better. And, again, I assure you this is a factual account. I experienced this event as clearly as I write it. (I think you can see why folks thought I was a tad looney, especially, in the first years, when I started crying and trembling as I recounted the story.)

Now, I soared on this current of energy through the pupil of this Eye and into the Universe at an unbelievable speed. The sensation was thrilling, yet I felt safe. We all know astronomers say the Universe is shooting outwards because of the original Big Bang Theory. Well, as the stars and galaxies scattered against the magnificent Ether were hurtling away from me, I felt part of the same motion. As I streamed toward them, they continued moving outward. I could feel the energy running through me, out my fingertips to the left and to the right. I felt euphoric. I felt calm, energized, free. For a moment, a wave of understanding washed over me. I understood everything. The meaning of Creation. The purpose of life. Why we are here. I remember saying, "Oh! It is all so simple. How could we not know?"

Why were we created? Why are we here? Simply: To experience Love. Without exception. We are the Creation of an outpouring of unlimited and unbridled Love. I'd say we are a manifestation, nay, an explosion of Love which occurred because *the joy of creating us could not be contained!*

This Being to whom I connected was (is) the purest, most innocent, and joyful form of Existence I have ever experienced. I felt as if this Presence cannot or will not comprehend hate, fear, unkindness, tragedy, violence, suffering, loss, depression, despondency, greed or lack. It registered with me that negative emotions such as these simply do not exist for this Being. At all. Not in the least.

Do you understand what I am saying? If I tried to explain a single negative expression to this Being, it would be as if He could not hear me. As if while expressing such earthly pain I would become invisible because for this Being, pain does not exist. Negativity is not a manifestation of God. Therefore, simply does not exist.

I am saying, Truth is Joy. Truth is Fearless. Truth is Innocence. Truth is Wisdom. These concepts are hard to conceive in today's difficult world. However, I saw that negative emotion simply does not exist in the realm of Perfection.

What we fail to understand is that we are a part of this Perfection. We were created as an outpouring of love from the sheer joy of creating. Each human being is a perfect machine (our humanity) carrying a perfect soul (our eternity). When we experience an event that we consider negative, there is positive behind it. There is no punishment from a deity, but a deeper lesson—of our own creation—to be derived for understanding love and how it is meant to work for us.

Ages ago, perhaps Adam and Eve (or the first human inhabitants of our world if Adam and Eve are not a part of your vernacular) chose to live separately from Perfection. Why? I have an idea, which I will share later in this work. But I believe that just as long ago our first progenitors chose to live separately from our Creator and taught this separate way of life as truth, we can just as easily choose to be united with our Creator once more, and fully live the Truth. In doing so, we rejoin the activity of perfect, constant Creation, which is why we were born.

Can you comprehend the possibility? We can live whole, abundant, fulfilling, joyful and fearless lives! It simply takes soul.

Now, continuing with my story, to top off this breathtaking experience, this Being spoke to me. I heard Him speak in a gentle and loving whisper in response to my interior terror. He said, "I am so gentle. I would never harm you."

Simply. In a whisper. Not what I expected to hear. (Actually, I hadn't expected to hear anything.) I felt so safe, I wanted to throw my arms up and leave with this

Being, never to return. I felt as if the choice was mine. But I suddenly remembered where I was, that I had recently married, and my husband and family would not know what happened to me. I said out loud, "They won't know what happened."

At my words, the Eye closed. And was gone. I sucked in a huge breath and opened my eyes to see I still stood in the church holding hands with my mother and brother. Knees trembling and near tears, I asked, "Did anyone see that?"

No one had. The experience was so overwhelming, it left me in shock. I can't remember much of what happened afterwards. My mother herded us all back into the car. Stunned from what I saw, I cried while trying to explain what had happened.

My mother must have believed she made a mistake taking us to the healing service because she decided we needed a distraction. She headed for Sturbridge Village in Massachusetts where the preserved village stands exactly as it existed as a colonial town in the 1600's. Her plan didn't help because we walked into the governor's home in this town and lo and behold, in the pristine dining room, where the table is perpetually set for an elegant meal, the curved ceiling over the host's seat depicted a mural of blue sky, white clouds, filled with cherubim and seraphim. In the center of all this splendor, a golden triangle with an opened Eye adorned the mural. I felt like I had been vindicated. I pointed to the ceiling and said, "Look! That is what I saw!"

Not sure what to do, my mother piled us into the car to head home. I don't know what she expected to happen on the visit to the charismatic healing, but she did not want her children to be hysterical with fear and pointing out visions they had no proof of experiencing.

The day was a bust for Mother but changed my life forever. I am happy to tell anyone willing to listen. Please read on so I may explain how this encounter awakened me to view the world from the eyes of my soul, which in turn gave me insight into who we are and why we are here.

CHAPTER THREE

The Stifling Power of Fear

From the distance of years since my encounter, I learned one thing most important: Fear is a four-letter word. Since the general population tends to believe there are certain four-letter words better left unspoken, I suggest we add Fear to the list.

Here is why: I didn't come away from that charismatic healing service frightened. I came away terrified. Awed, enlightened, but terrified. My intellect was overwhelmed, and my ego threatened, because neither could process what I had witnessed. Due to this confusion fueled by fear, I quickly discovered I was better off remaining silent. Why? As previously mentioned, when I attempted to explain the experience,

I broke down into a blubbering mess. Crying. Shaking. As you can imagine, I made folks uncomfortable. I couldn't get over the fact that I had seen, felt and understood an immense, love-fueled power so alien to the earth-bound existence I knew. By reacting to my fear, I stifled my drive to share.

Perhaps you may wonder why I behaved this way? Several factors. First, the experience was so overpowering, it defied reality. In many ways, it could be likened to your possible reaction if you encountered a visitor from another planet for the first time. I'd bet the experience would leave you rather jittery, to say the least! Additionally, think of how difficult it would be to get others to believe you.

My connection with the Holy Spirit had a significantly greater wallop. While exquisitely wonderful, yet frightening in intensity, I could not explain the phenomenon—and neither could anyone else. I approached several priests with whom I had a good rapport and they either had no answer or dismissed me with concern for my credibility.

Imagine my relief when I recounted my experience to my father, Herby. He pointed out that the eye I described is printed on the back of a United States one dollar bill. I was thrilled to see the United States of America saw fit to put such a symbol on our currency.

The dollar bill, as well as the mural in Sturbridge, helped justify I was not the first person to know about such an image. But honestly, what I saw was indescribably more beautiful than the symbol on the dollar. I felt like the artist did not recreate the true power and magnificence I experienced. And, while I understand this symbol has its own name and meaning, I cannot give the Holy Spirit this name, because He is indescribable.

So, even with my father's willingness to believe me, I still could not recount the experience calmly, and my emotional descriptions distressed others. The few times I had told people in the early days, their incredulous reactions were the same. (When carpooling with a co-worker, she threatened to make me get out of her car if I continued telling my story.) And I was embarrassing my husband. People thought I was nuts—just as most folks do when someone relates an encounter with an UFO—except my story was on steroids! I needed to be liked, not rejected. So, I kept my story to myself.

In the ensuing years, I spent endless hours contemplating the event. A new appreciation for people, and the world around me, had infused my being. My world view grew sweeter, more compassionate, more appreciative of everything I did. With family, friends, and every person I encountered, I spoke to their souls through my soul. It may have been the simplest of conversations, but they knew I spoke genuinely. How?

Because their souls felt my intent to interact from a place of love, many times probably unknowingly. One can recognize a soul discussion best when they walk away saying something akin to, "what a great conversation", or "I feel as though I was understood," or "I feel that we accomplished a wonderful outcome."

Don't misunderstand me. Living soulfully does not exclude human emotion. Anger, sadness, joy, etc., are part of our humanity, but when these emotions are ego driven, they are singular, personal points of view uncaring of others; when soul driven, those involved in the moment become connected with each other. Whether there is agreement or not, all reactions are honored, explored, understood, accepted, rejected, or celebrated while still maintaining one's dignity.

Once you become more soul aware, many wonderful experiences begin to happen—or have happened in the past that you did not recognize as soul channeled. Some call the events coincidence, others luck. I have found this hard-to-explain experience is the flow of God's energy working through us. One easy example is when you find yourself thinking about someone and the phone rings. Or sadly, someone you love passes away, and you sense this—or have a dream about this person—before you are told. You can call it telepathy, but the conduit is the soul.

Another example for me was the birth of my two sons. I truly understood the miracle of life behind their creation and consciously participated with their growth while carrying them.

Each time I realized I was pregnant I asked my unborn children their names. Both times, they told me. (The answers were like a flash in my mind.) Daniel, then Evan. Both males were born and have grown up true to their names. Coincidences? Lucky guesses? Possibly. But I consciously communicated with the souls I carried, and believed they answered.

For me, the gifts of time and life experience became the remedies for the initial dread I felt from encountering the Holy Spirit. Through the years, my choices to make decisions and interact with others as a soul-driven channel of God brought real time results and the impetus to teach others. I also concluded that during those unfortunate times when I accepted, rather than rejected fear, I mistrusted my own judgement and let my ego drive my decisions—ultimately becoming mistaken, and then chastising myself for my inadequacies. When I dismissed fear, I regained the power to obtain my intentions and succeeded.

During those precious moments with the Holy Spirit, I initially did not understand my place in the presence of this enormous Power. I had become frightened by the Holy Spirit's overwhelming love that was far greater than my intellect could handle. The enormity of that Being's energy not only terrified me but left me awestruck. The Holy Spirit shared Himself with my soul and I lived to tell the story. Wow! So, I know, right down to my soul, telling my story is what I am supposed to do.

To best describe the Holy Spirit, I suggest imagining a mountain of burning energy, like a white-hot star, alive, intelligent, self-contained, and immense with power. (Reference the Old Testament description of Moses and the Burning Bush. Exodus 3:2-6. *And the Lord appeared to him in a flame of fire out of the midst of a bush…*) For those folks not familiar with this passage, here is an excerpt from an article written by a theologian named David T. Adamo,[1] who discusses this event as a natural phenomenon contrasted across different natural/cultural interpretations:

"…Since the days of Philo of Alexandria, this passage has been given a nationalistic interpretation representing the Hebrew/Jews protection for their suffering in Egypt and Babylon. It was also suggested that it represents the Holy Spirit, Jesus Christ and even Virgin Mary and the church. Although the event was also interpreted to represent the sun, it has been said to be a hallucination because of drugs in the wilderness. It has even become several names of churches and seminaries. However, many have hit the

nail on the head by interpreting it as God's self-disclosure or the presence of the divinity…"

In this same work, Adamo also adds,

"When Moses asks the name of the speaker, the speaker revealed his name to Moses. This name was translated as 'Yahweh' of which its traditional connection is the verb meaning 'to exist'. The name is regarded as the supreme name of God and the highest disclosure of the divine nature to humanity…"

I suppose I missed my opportunity to definitively establish the name of this amazing presence by asking his name, as Moses did. The thought never occurred to me because I knew I was witnessing God the Father through the Holy Spirit, whom I invoked when I became terrified.

In addition, the presence I witnessed was no manageable-sized bush. I felt minuscule in size compared to this awesome presence. This Being, with His fire and energy, was so capable of extinguishing me, that afterwards, my primal reaction was terror.

As an analogy, imagine walking in a field on a beautiful day when a thunderbolt strikes from nowhere, leaving a huge smoldering crater at your feet. Imagine your reaction as you realize you could have been obliterated. In contrast, while more impactful that a thunderbolt, the Presence I experienced exuded nothing but gentleness, love, intelligence, and joy. He seemed genuinely thrilled to relate to me! Can you imagine such generosity? I sensed an unfathomable intellect possessing innocence, overwhelming love and a playfulness that left me feeling giddy.

This entity of explosive bridled energy so full of power and brilliance, while completely charged with joy, kindness, and—God bless Him—innocence, could never conceive of doing harm to me, anyone, or anything. The dichotomy of such overwhelming power coupled with this Being's ignorance of cruelty confounded my senses.

The Holy Spirit had no responsibility to make Himself known to me but chose to do so because He heard my terror and wanted to put me at ease. He did so by showing me His Universe, like an exuberant child introducing his playground to a new kid in the neighborhood. Only, this Being was mature, soft spoken and intelligent beyond comprehension.

My first revelation after the experience was this: I understood the true meaning behind the biblical words, *"Fear of the Lord is the beginning of wisdom. Prov. 1-7."*

Fear of the Lord was never meant to be punitive, as in, Fear God or He will punish you. No! No! Fear the

Lord means that we perfect and beautiful humans are so very microscopic in understanding and structure in comparison to His Existence (as compared to one single cell vs. our entire body) that we could be destroyed simply by proximity. Like standing on Ground Zero when an atom bomb detonates. I don't know about you, but a being of such immensity most certainly earns my love, awe, and respect. Especially because the earned wisdom increases our love for Him as we absorb into our own body, mind, and soul that not one destructive, unkind, or unloving atom exists in the structure of God—his Holy Spirit. God will never harm us. Hence, our fear transforms into understanding.

I met God during this encounter. In the form of Holy Spirit or Telepathic Union? I don't know. I do know I could have died a happy woman and been welcome into conscious, creative, perfect bliss. Forever.

It is important to understand that while created as individuals, we remain a part of God—like within our bodies, every different atom with its own memory and intelligence (imagine yourself as a single cell) exists to make us one whole body of existence—which is God. So, if this Being from whom we are created has no fear, then, why should we? Rather, why not tap back into our tie to Him through our souls and achieve our life's journey with wisdom, kindness, joy, peace?

Coming to this conclusion, I became disappointed with the dogma of so many of today's religions. I saw rules of God designed, or perhaps misinterpreted, by men to achieve more earthly goals rather than living to attain Heaven, or in this life, attain Heaven on Earth. I saw the rules and demands of many religions losing their traditional spiritual wisdom to engendered political biases that have nothing to do with the Love of God. Hence, the root of frustration for many religious devotees whose vocation to spread God's Word becomes ham-strung by dogmatic red tape and rules that continue to change as societies change.

There is only one Rule: Love. Love of God. Love thy neighbor as thyself. In him or her, as in you, will you find your strength, the gift of God: the power of Love. All else flows from this.

If what I have written upsets you, consider your reaction's source. Anger and anxiety results from fear rising in the ego—or your sense of self. I may have challenged a structure or a set of rules by which you may have built your world to feel safe. But, if your world is correct, what I say has no bearing and should not upset your intellect, or your emotional safety. Emotional safety is a product of fear. If fear did not exist, neither would emotional safety, because there would be no emotional harm from which we need protection. In other words, anything anyone may say has no bearing on your core existence when your spiritual and intellectual foundation is sound. Therefore, ego-generated fear is unnecessary.

Fear, not greed, is the root of evil. Greed is a product of fear. And I dislike using the word, evil, at all. However, in the English language, the word evil means *anything morally wrong or bad, causing injury or harm*. Now, take the word evil and spell it backwards. What do you get? LIVE!

Coincidence? Who knows? But it makes my point. The absence of evil brings life. Fullness. Blossoming. Joy. If our world existed without fear, there would be no evil.

The answer is that simple.

Ha! You say. Never happen. To that, I say, Ha! I believe in miracles. I also believe in the power of the Human Spirit made in the image and likeness of God.

You and I may most surely agree that everything we witness in today's news, whether reporting on global, political and/or economic forces, wars, medical emergencies, racial commentaries, rampant crimes, natural disasters, mass destruction of human life either born or unborn, pushes fear deep into our psyche, as intended. This is all a manifestation of evil—that which uses cognizant, ego-driven terror to achieve a goal.

Why, as a society, do why accept this as a fact of life? The apparent motives of power and greed seem insane!

Again, if we were to awaken, one by one, to the uselessness of fear-based thinking, then one by one we would tap into our personal, soul-driven talents to fuel our intellects and live fearlessly. But that will not happen until we, as a species, consciously choose to engage our souls as our compass.

Our souls are our link to God's perfection. We don't think enough from our souls. Our ego dominates most of our actions and our ego is fear based. The concept behind the new age law of attraction comes close but doesn't quite hit the mark for achieving life purposes. The soul is the conduit for this attraction, yet the ego takes control of the idea of the law of attraction and believes "it" is the secret attractor of abundance. This understanding is erroneous, and results are not achieved.

What is the ego? The Merriam-Webster dictionary defines ego as, *the self especially as contrasted with another self or the world; the one of the three divisions of the psyche in psychoanalytical theory that serves as the organized conscious mediator between the person and reality, especially by functioning both in the perception of and adaptation to reality.*

The Cambridge Dictionary says *the ego is your idea or opinion of yourself, especially your feeling of your own importance and ability. In psychoanalysis, the part of a person's mind that tries to match hidden desires (= wishes) of the ID (= part of the unconscious mind) with the demands of the real world.*

Precious as the ego is for showing our uniqueness, it restricts us from tapping into our soul to understand our connection to each other, the earth, the universe, because it sees itself as separate and threatened. Thoughts becoming things from an ego-generated source tend to eventually backfire from any good results gained.

Like the third side of an equilateral triangle, our soul binds ego and intellect, the other two gifts—or tools—and makes us whole. When all three tools are employed, the law of attraction begins through our soul. Thoughts then become things for our good, and the good of others.

Our soul is the conduit for creation. While ego manifests the original vision for abundance by igniting our individual talents, the soul channels the power from our Creator. Once manifested, the intellect brings the vision to fruition. The missing link (or the unspoken secret) has been to actively engage the soul to open and allow Creation's flow in the creative process. Success requires trust, or faith, in the fact the soul process exists.

Trust your instincts. Trust your intellect. Trust your body. Every inch of you, mind, body, and soul are your learning tools. Use them to find your answers. The search for Truth is an adventure. However, the Truth cannot be found when fear is involved.

Let's take a moment to define fear. The American Psychological Association defines fear as:

n. a basic, intense emotion aroused by the detection of imminent threat, involving an immediate alarm reaction that mobilizes the organism by triggering a set of physiological changes . . . Some propose that fear is experienced when avoiding or escaping an aversive stimulus and that anxiety is experienced when entering a potentially dangerous situation (e.g., an animal foraging in a field where there might be a predator). Whatever their precise differences in meaning, however, the terms are often used interchangeably in common parlance.

Fear has been inbred into the human condition as a part of life and has its service. I'm not saying stand fearlessly in front of a train or charging lion. To remove yourself from physical danger is common sense in saving your precious life. And rational anxiety for doing something correctly before an important event can be an excellent motivator to achieve the moment. My point is that when interacting with our fellow human beings for enjoyment, business, education, politics, etc., fully aware of our soulful presence, intellectual capacity, and without fear, we would achieve results through strength, compassion, curiosity, and love.

Think of how you are so surprised when a stranger makes a gesture of good will on your behalf. You tell your friends about it. Why? Because in many cases today, kindness has become neglected.

Think of how ego-generated fear (remember, fear generates greed, mistrust, and the obsession for power) established the benchmark driving the history of all wars, including the twentieth century's World Wars and the Holocaust, Russia's Civil War, the Irish War of Independence, Spanish Civil War, the Partition of India, the on-going Israeli-Palestinian Conflict, the Vietnam War, etc., totaling twenty-eight recorded wars/conflicts throughout that century! The twenty first century is already littered with concluded and ongoing conflicts and continuing global terrorism.

The belief that there is not enough for survival (or prosperity) sends countries grasping for control of other nations and their resources. Until every single human being consciously chooses to believe the possibility that there is enough for all, and that there is beauty to be found in the world's myriad cultures and traditions, this horrendous cycle of abuse will continue.

I believe we can eradicate fear, the one destructive source on this planet, person by person. Day in and day out. The only requirement is to trust you are safe. When you react wrongly, try again. The first place to begin eradicating fear in our lives is to understand and trust there are enough earthly resources to go around on this sustaining, ever renewing and perfect planet to accommodate everything that lives.

Fearlessness creates a ripple effect in generosity, understanding and love. Those emotions become the norm when fear is absent. The organic (survival mode) belief that there is not enough—we are not enough—to sustain our own lives stops us from trusting ourselves and others. When fear is removed, we trust our own talent(s), take the risks to become who we were born to be, and rejoice in our own and everyone else's success. Now, read on to learn how simple it is to engage the soul to achieve these goals.

1   Adamo, David T. (2017). The Burning Bush (Ex 3:1-6): A study of natural phenomena as manifestation of divine presence in the Old Testament and in African context. HTS Theological Studies, 73(3), 1-8. https://dx.doi.org/10.4102/hts.v73i3.4576

CHAPTER FOUR

Engaging the Soul

When we consciously awaken to the existence of our soul, we become aware of our connection to everything and everyone we see and cannot see. A tree, a rock, a river, a bird, or another person takes on an impression of life we never noticed. With fear removed, we become comfortable knowing that which we cannot understand will eventually become clear. With soul thinking, seeking knowledge brings clearer insights. We are not meant to be solitary beings. Soul thinking gathers us to each other. Everyone has inborn gifts we are meant to share with each other, in all avenues of life.

As I mentioned previously, to understand and use this in-born gift of our soul, which we already possess, is to unleash the power to be who we were born to be. Once this awareness opens and fear diminishes, our curiosity heightens. We become more inclined to celebrate ourselves, everyone, and everything in our lives.

Individuality does not separate us from each other but outlines our part as one of the incalculable and unique threads weaving the entire tapestry of Creation. This new awareness from the soul binds us to each other. Where our soul is our spiritual life source, soul thinking awakens our awareness to the earth as our physical life-source. The earth is our playground. Our nurturer. Our performing stage. We understand the earth has evolved to perfectly suit our physical needs with all the proper elements for life. And likewise, the earth serves our spiritual needs by offering her flawless and magnificent beauty and sustaining grace to leave us in awe. This is our gift from our Creator. Isn't that wonderful?

How does one begin soul thinking?

First, simply accept the fact your soul exists. Think of the soul as another organ of the body, like our heart or our lungs. Sit quietly for a moment and probe inwards. Acknowledge your soul and ask it to work for you. I would not be surprised if you felt a tingling throughout your body as you greet your soul, and it ignites at your recognition.

With your heart and lungs, you feel a pulse and an inhaled breath. You know your body is chorded with nerve endings and veins, because medical science explains this fact. We've also seen tons of medical studies to prove the existence of electrochemical activity in the body, but we cannot see this process without the aid of technology.

Here is where the soul becomes dismissed. We cannot see it, nor detect it with technology. So, it is considered a possibility, or a reality depending on your beliefs, and most believe the soul is of no use until death. For this reason, the soul has been little attended, except through religion and mysticism.

This next fact is crucial: Our soul exists for use now, just as our organs exist for use now. I cannot emphasize this truth enough. Our souls originate from the same life-source of creation that brought us into the world. While your physical umbilical cord to your mother was severed at birth, the soul, as a spiritual umbilical cord, remains connected to our original source of life. The continued connection to Creation gives us endless possibilities which manifest as imagination and thought.

Since we cannot see this source, and there has been no scientific proof, some tend to believe the soul, or its power as a tool, does not exist. This is where faith comes in. Do you remember the American movie, "Field of Dreams" with Kevin Costner? A voice whispered, "If you build it, they will come." Same with the soul. If you believe in your soul, your soul will perform for you. The soul always responds. Whether or not we acknowledge our soul determines its effectiveness. Keven Costner's character would not have built the controversial baseball field that threatened the credibility of his sanity, and the financial stability of his home, if he didn't trust what his soul told him, despite all the criticism he received.

Our soul is the spiritual organ within us that grants access to power far greater than our intellect can carry us. Simply put, our soul is our conduit to God, the source of our creation, and continues to remain open to us as a source for creating!

This is not a religious statement. This is a fact of truth shared with me by the Holy Spirit. I know. Another outrageous claim. The fact is when fear-based intellect is employed, our connection to divine creation stops—like crimping a hose to stop the water flow.

Remember, I felt terror (from lack of understanding) when those people in that church were dropping around me. I begged God not to expose me to what I perceived as dangerous to my existence. The Holy Spirit dispelled my fear, and did so as only God would, spectacularly! That momentary bond through my soul connection

showed me there is no place for fear in the Universe.
(By the way, I give "Him" a male gender because he
appeared and sounded masculine—and OMG, I miss
the sound of his voice!)

It makes no difference whether, or not, one chooses
to accept the soul as our direct connection to God or
Creation. The soul exists no matter what one believes.
An ignored soul simply remains an untapped source of
energy which will return to source when our bodies are
finished. There is no other way. Energy, once created,
cannot be destroyed.[1] Science proves this fact. And we
cannot ignore the fact we were created. Look down at
your hands and see . . . There you are.

So, if you choose to become aware of your soul, you
will feel it come alive. You will feel calmer. Fear will
begin to evaporate. You may become bolder in your
decisions. More confident. Your concerns will seem
less threatening because you will understand all will
become as it should.

Our souls shimmer with the essence of our ability
to channel love and create, using our chosen talents.
This source remains open to us in our waking lives and
in our dreams. This untapped energy is endless. Soul
thinking turns competition into co-creating; bigotry
into curiosity; anger into compassion; envy into delight
in another's abilities to create. The more used, the more

soul thinking opens our awareness with fearless strength and unbounded joy.

Is this resonating within you? Does it make sense? I hope so!

The first, single-most important point I absorbed from my experience is, *You and I are the product of sublime and extraordinary love.* Please read that sentence again. I did not choose those words lightly. You and I were created because the thought of you and me alive in the world as unique channels for God to continue Creation was so exciting and generated such a passionate blast of emotion, our souls exploded into existence. Like the creation of a star. Can you understand from this description how important you are? It's mind-boggling!

Secondly, I learned the futility of that stupid—yes, I said stupid—four-letter word: Fear. I acknowledge that fear initiated my encounter with this Being, and fear silenced me for all these years after seeing adverse reactions. But, with time, I grasped the experience in its entirety. Fear stalled my delivery of this important information. However, in the end, I am grateful. The gift of time granted me the full understanding of what I had experienced. That said, I declare completely and wholeheartedly that *fear is the biggest scam on earth*.

Let's go deeper . . .

What if fear was eliminated from our existence? Impossible? Hmm. I think the possibility exists. Sure, as an evolved species, the flight or fight instinct still rests deeply imbedded in our DNA. Folks suffer phobias and fears too numerous to discuss here. But as evolving humans, where fear was a tool used to stay alive, consider this: What if we, as a species, have evolved intellectually and spiritually enough to eliminated fear as a tool for our existence? I'm not discounting common sense reactions to danger. That is different. But the approach to dangers, natural and man-made, can be approached with a sense of fearlessness.

This is why:

During my encounter, I understood right down to my core that Fear does not exist at all for the Being who connected with me. I know, you may say, well, of course. God is God. Why should he be afraid of anything? But again, let me repeat in different terms, just as you are created from your parents' genetic makeup—you know, she has her mother's eyes; he has his father's disposition—so are we a creation of the stuff of the Universe, or our Creator. If He is fearless, then it is within us to be the same.

Think of the craze we have for superheroes. (My favorite is Superman.) Could it be we are recognizing our own, untapped potential? I am thinking, yes. Our admiration of superhero excellence and amazing powers is our soul recognizing its own ability and tapping at our awareness. I believe fear not only halts our forward motion to success, peace, and happiness, but once more, I suggest fear keeps us from becoming superheroes!

Emotional fear is the brainchild of our ego—another invisible force within us functioning primarily for our primitive survival. The ego's goal? To keep itself safe from "danger" at all costs—even at the expense of the self, and others. (I jokingly say, like a monkey with a machine gun in our heads.)

The ego triggers a primal protection mechanism by instilling fear in each of us. But today, despite all our technology, medical advancements, education and ease of living, the ego continues to generate fear, when fear is virtually no longer needed, because we can create solutions for practically everything.

Fear manifests itself in a broad spectrum, from raw reaction to the most sophisticated thought. I believe we, as humans, have evolved enough to rely less on the ego and more on our souls. It is time to remove chaos caused by ego and instill perfection by thinking and creating from a soul-based platform.

Again, I'm not talking about fear of falling, or fear of fire. Those are instinctual and intelligent responses for keeping our bodies safe and whole. I'm talking about fear of knowledge. Fear of failure. Fear of success. Fear of the unknown. Fear of a stranger, the dark, spiders, flying. You get my meaning. What began as an instinctual survival method has morphed into a way of life. Why? Because just like the soul, the ego is a living entity within us wishing to survive.

With this scientific knowledge of the ego and its behavior, I find it overwhelmingly shocking that while knowing what they are doing, today's newscasters and media sources bombard the airways with biased, fear-based news reporting which does nothing but create panic and rage. Again, I ask, to what end does this fearmongering serve? Does it serve you? Your children? Your grandchildren?

The answer is an overwhelming, no.

Again, I want to emphasize that the ego is another primal tool which helps us recognize our unique selves. Our talents. Our dreams. Our goals and desires. The ego is one of Freud's psychological triplets to human behavior: Id (primitive motivator), Ego (sense of self) and Super Ego (conscience) [2]).

However, we have given our egos free reign and they have run amuck. Unlike the soul, the ever-critical ego, as a living entity, will survive at the cost of your happiness. And it usually does. I once heard an excellent acronym for EGO: Easing God Out. That says it all.

The clever ego battles to stay alive. It stays alive and grows stronger by making us feel separate from our souls, from ourselves and from each other. Worse, it fosters the idea of enemies. This is not intentional; it is an unconscious survival impulse of an internal entity that duels with one's intelligence, conscience, and the reality of life.

Where the soul sees the planet as an integral extension of the individual, the ego views the planet as an inexhaustible resource for individual needs and pleasure. Do you see the difference? The former nurtures while the latter absorbs.

The ego makes us feel separated and alone, while creating the craving to be connected to others. The ego is our worse critic. It builds us up, then knocks us down with self-doubt. It keeps us grasping at love, happiness, wealth, and success, but leaves us empty when we've achieved these goals—or worse, when we don't. When this happens, it is because ego and intellect are used to achieve needs without employing the soul—the third wall of the triangle for perfection.

Now, understand this: like God, the loving and gentle soul respects Free Will and steps aside to accommodate the over-active ego. Think of the ego as the loudest, rudest person in the room, while the soul is the person with the most impeccable manners. Where the soul recognizes Free Will, the ego does not. The greatest battle you will have in employing soul thinking will be in harnessing your ego enough to acknowledge the soul exists. To harness the ego, one must engage the intellect to recognize that the ego is actively protecting itself, or in other words, criticizing, complaining, judging, self-aggrandizing.

To employ soul thinking, your ego will have to be trained by the intellect to respect your Free Will (the second precious gift of humanity). The ego has no plans of letting go, until through conscious effort and reasoning away emotional fear, you demand that the ego remains still. And it will, because once the fear that drives the ego to act evaporates, the ego will no longer feel threatened, and settle down.

Once again, I am not dismissing the ego. The ego, also a creation of God, helps us recognize our inner talents, and foster our intelligence with the drive to achieve. But the ego has become more important than the soul because it delivers tangible results through emotion and logic. The soul requires faith and understanding. Without proof of its existence, the soul gets rejected and the ego remains dominant.

Why? Because throughout human history, actions of the ego generated, and continue to generate, material wealth, intellectual achievement, and positions of power on small to grand scales. However, to date, without employing the soul, the fruits of the ego and the intellect also succumbed to self-doubt, fear, suspicion, pomposity, and greed, causing political and economic chaos, and wars with disregard for human life and the earth's resources. So many of today's success stories leave their creators unhappy, seeking more than they have achieved both personally and financially, and in worse case, as we've witnessed with celebrities, resulting in death from addiction, irrational behavior, and suicide.

Humanity has created countless wonderful inventions while generating growth and wealth throughout the ages. However, using the ego and intellect without soul thinking has tainted most progress by accepting environmentally damaging bi-products, human destruction, and the drive to control. The soul will not permit such actions. It might take a bit more thinking and strategizing to progress soulfully with inventions and growth, but the outcome would benefit everyone.

Now, I'm not talking about creating communism or socialism, or any political denomination that either does or does not exist. With soul thinking, the world would not require political parties. The world would require a genuine desire by humanity to reach peace and prosperity as a common goal—in whatever ways nations and individuals contribute their talents.

Not everyone has the same talents, dreams, and aspirations, but everyone has something to offer. There is monetary and spiritual value to talent, be it in fields of science, technology, medicine, farming, education, recreation, commerce, entertainment, construction, engineering, land husbandry, ad infinitum. In soul-based thinking there is always someone out there who can supply what you need—and vice versa. It is a matter of community and contribution. There are no cut corners or free rides. Everyone responsibly attends to the steps required to achieve the success they seek. With soul-based thinking, there is no jealousy in another's achievements but an excitement in helping others reach their goals by contributing, and in return, receiving support. The results? We celebrate each other's success and prosper energetically, responsibly, and profitably. I know this sounds impossible, but I promise you. This symbiotic model to existence is why we were born. We've simply been missing the power of the soul to complete the formula for perfecting our life experience.

The ego is threatened by soul thinking. Where the soul unites us, the ego sets us apart. The ego makes one believe he or she is more important than another. The ego invites the fear-driven vices that keep society in chaos:

greed, avarice, envy, bigotry, lust, violence . . . to name a few. Let me remind you: all these vices germinate from fear. When we fear a lack of success, love, or power, the next human response is to compete, over-indulge, mistrust and control. And, in worse cases, attack.

The science of psychology took time and experimenting to prove the ego's existence, so now, the ego is accepted as a true emotional/mental state. However, the soul and its power as a human factor, or a tool for creation, continues to go unconfirmed. Goodness is usually taken for granted. And since the soul's existence cannot be scientifically proven, for now, only faith and trust make it so. Ironically, faith and trust in the power of God acting through us, are the easiest methods to achieve success, love, and contentment, because all we need do is Believe, Act, and be Grateful. (I like to say, it's all in the BAG.)

Here is where fear is a scam. To thrive, the ego uses fear as the most potent means to keep us (and itself) safe. The ego whispers the heady belief that we, because of our individual talents or beliefs, are better than those who are not like us. The ego insists our individual needs take precedence over another's, be it a loved one or a stranger.

Worse, the ego fosters that a person who looks or thinks differently from us is dangerous, because they threaten our own identity. Fear has brought us the troubles facing today's society. In politics, religion, cultural beliefs, education and families, the ego makes humanity feel important enough to dominate others, even reducing to violence, to keep individual beliefs alive and most of all, safe.

Many times, believing to "know what is best" gives an excuse to dominate others. Again, knowing what is best, is another way to insure all is safe in one's own world. Insisting that others follow one's rules ensures one's personal comfort. This behavior is why the all-trusting soul has been completely subordinated by fear, and the ego dominates today's cultures.

For example, control and fearmongering reared its ugly head during the Covid19 pandemic in 2020. The media assaults presented at the outbreak of this pandemic, with unsubstantiated facts about this mysterious and unknown illness, caused instant panic and chaos. World leaders and medical professionals who courageously used their souls, intellect, and Free Will to state what they scientifically understood to be the best solutions to corralling the pandemic and saving lives, were either silenced, fired, or dismissed from media attention in favor of the initial actions taken in isolating people, and shutting down business and industry.

While drastic measures needed to be employed to stop the spreading disease, fear drove the most unreasonable demands and solutions that were used—creating terror, distrust, and disrespect among people. Unnecessary strife both in loss of life and economic decline resulted from the fear-instilled demands made "law" in many locations. While the cause for this outbreak remains unknown, there are assumptions ranging from infection from bats to viral warfare. We may never know the answer. And a mystery such as this creates fear in the form of conspiracy theories, mistrust in our "experts", and the frustrating inability to believe what is reported in the media. So where is there a reliable and truthful source of information on which we can depend in a crisis, when presently, there is censoring and false news? A soul-based society would never reach such dismal proportions. I am curious to see what the history books will say about global human behavior during this calamitous world event.

I heard a saying once in relation to fiction writing and screenplays: Even the villain is a hero in his own mind. Regarding warfare, it is well known that laboratories around the world experiment with deadly chemical and viral agents. Perhaps world leaders, scientists, and medical researchers driven to experiment with and/or employ deadly chemical and viral agents for whatever purposes, believe their work heroic? That would be a generous explanation to an abysmal mindset. I question the heroics behind the experimentation with deadly agents that if used to achieve some so-called greater good could result in harm to human beings, animals, and the planet.

These questionably altruistic, ego-driven motives to experiment with deadly diseases and contaminants are derived not from a desire to improve the world, but from a primal fear to keep safe those initiating the experimentation. Period. This mindset uses intelligence and ego to play God for personal gain. There is no holiness in such motives. Just because we have the wherewithal to create a monster, does not mean we should. A soul-driven, intellectual being will recognize this fact and choose another path.

Like the layers of an onion, we must peel back through the ages to determine the origin of the first fear-based action to harm another for one's own survival and safety. Fast-forwarding to today's uber-advanced, technological capabilities, assaults on our world in every human aspect are more widespread and deadlier than any time in history; all because the primal, soulless, egoic drive to stay safe has been given free reign through the centuries.

Again, the ego creates insecurities, along with angry and negative thoughts and actions which undermine trust, confidence, self-love, and safely calculated risks.

By dominating what is becoming the world's conscious mind, the world ego has become humanity's Achille's Heel. With the continuation of wars, global pandemics, and acts of terrorism, chances of decent human survival become more and more questionable. So much time is spent in dispelling chaos, defending personal dignity, and rebuilding lives, that simple day-to-day peaceful living and production of goods for consumption are lost.

I believe that if we encourage each other to recognize and ignite the soul in making choices, more and more people will teach the ego to quiet, and the desired effect to reach cooperative solutions in every aspect of life would spread faster and be more welcome globally than today's destructive behaviors.

It all begins by simply saying, "No," to chaos.

Doesn't it sound better to allow the soul to tap the source of our talent with love, excitement, and generosity, instead of ego generated fear, suspicion, and greed? With no fear of lack, or that someone will steal what is ours, criticize us, or instill shame, we are free to help ourselves and each other towards individual prosperity. Celebrating each other's talents is to create the tapestry of life as intended on earth: perfect symmetry.

Now, you may be thinking, perfection is impossible. There is always something wrong somewhere. Gangs. Serial killers. Natural disasters. Famine. War mongers. Physical and emotional strife. Corporate and cultural criminals. Yes. These exist. Is there no wonder that violence, considered by so many as necessary for survival, has become more measured and sophisticated in today's world?

Yet to contrast this negativity, I say humanity can reach perfection. I believe soul thinking is an evolutionary process to which we have arrived. Many wonderful things are happening today, which deserve our focus. We are witnessing the emergence of innovative, environmentally conscious leaders of industry, and all avenues of life-embracing mission statements that encourage loyalty and growth for all involved while employing new techniques to keep the planet clean, and those around them happy with their choices. These innovators recognize humanity's mistakes and have become progressive with new inventions and technology, while encouraging employees and competitors to co-create in their industries.

I believe the younger generations are naturally becoming soul thinkers from sheer need. They see what prior generations have done wrong and are actively responding for better choices. I see soul thinking emerging more and more in toddlers and children.

All the wonderful, awe-inspiring happenings in the world are coming from today's soul thinkers. Only, I'll bet most of them don't even know their soul is the corridor they are tapping to create these new and humane solutions.

Imagine if everyone consciously tapped into their soul to aid their thinking? We would achieve our personal perfection and live our lives through perfection—as was intended. Even if doubt is tugging at your thoughts on these ideas, I'll bet you can feel the truth. Our souls are gifts ready to serve at any age, to accomplish every talent we were born to share, immediately.

So again, I suggest humanity, as a species, has evolved. (Explained more in the next chapter.) It is no longer necessary to attend the ego which drove the behaviors that created evil, for lack of a better word. Soul thinking is the new evolution to create the world we all desire. Loving. Fearless. Strong. Successful. Clean. Joyful. Exciting. Beautiful. All it takes is you, and your awakened soul, from today onward. Like dominoes falling in a line, the energy emanating from you will inspire those around you, simply by being your soulful self. It's the power of one, then another, then another—the single threads that weave together the tapestry of life.

Kathleen Ann Pickering

1   https://www.britannica.com/science/principles-of-physical-science/Conservation-of-mass-energy#ref366373

2   Sigmund Freud quote: "One might compare the relation of the ego to the id that will be between a rider and his horse. The horse provides the locomotor energy, and the rider has the prerogative of determining the goal and of guiding the movements of the powerful mount. . . The poor ego has a still harder time of it: it must serve three harsh masters and do its best to reconcile the demands of all three . . . the external world, the superego and the id." –From New Introductory Lectures on Psycho-Analysis, 1933

CHAPTER FIVE

The Evolution of Soul Thinking

I use the term, soul thinking, because as I described in previous chapters, I experienced my encounter with the Holy Spirit through my soul, all those years ago. My body stayed in place as my soul took flight. I learned, simply and immediately that my soul is physically real and the answer to everything lay in seeing the world through the eyes of my soul. Or, in other words, through the eyes of Love.

History's greatest spiritual teachers, and today's spiritual teachers employed, and continue to employ soul thinking in their approach to happiness and success in the world. I want to emphasize that the soul is not a passive or altruistic concept, but a powerful tool through which we are meant to act, now!

Let's take a minute to honor our body—the incredible complex machine in which we exist. Consider the trillions of unique and constantly renewing cells, the electro-chemical reactions on so many levels, nerve endings, sensory organs, working organs all governed by the amazing and mysterious brain, and functioning on their own with little input from us except for care and nourishment. Our bodies are perfect miracles. Another God-given gift.

Now, imagine this perfect miracle as the car your soul drives. An awesome machine. What a combination of miracle and grace! Now, add the soul as the driver, the intellect riding shotgun, and the ego in the back seat. Think of the joy, excitement, and fearless sense of adventure a body would experience driving through life with the peaceful soul as captain, the intellect absorbing all there is to learn, and the ego applying this information to enhance one's personal talents.

Only, most of today's miracle machines are manned in reverse: the ego in the driver's seat, with the intellect still riding shotgun, and the soul, oh, I don't know, maybe in the trunk? One literally sees this behavior on the roads today manifesting as road rage. So, how can our miracle bodies function as intended, when the ego is constantly jamming on the breaks or speeding unheeded through human traffic?

When soul-driven, the intellect sharpens. Mind and body function clearly, making more fruitful choices. On the other hand, the ego sees everyone else as in its way and causes disruption. Simply adding soul calms the situation, and completes the perfect trilateral use of soul, intellect, and ego, required to contribute properly to the world we were born to create. I find it fascinating that the missing link to humanity's success already resides within us! Simply adding the soul as a barometer in ego and intellect decision making, creates the complete vehicle which drives human perfection.

Once we truly understand our soul's purpose as an active tool for use in our lives, the puzzle pieces to enhancing so many economic, societal, and ecological concerns fit into place.

Viewing life through the eyes of Love does not make one weak, submissive, or unable to function powerfully in business or society. On the contrary, conducting life through soul thinking means decisions come from courage, wisdom, and clear vision, which replace ego-based motives, such as fear, greed, and/or a need to win at another's expense.

Once again, conducting life with courage, wisdom and compassion generates intellect, satisfaction, and prosperity to whatever degree a person desires. Success is good. Profit is good. A bountiful earth is good. The difference between success and profit earned with most of today's business models, and success and profit earned through soul thinking, is that through soul thinking, everyone prospers, and no one loses—including the planet. I call it, DIG. Conduction life with Dignity, Integrity, and Grace.

I was fascinated by the reactions of several accomplished entrepreneurs when I suggested soul thinking as the missing link to successful, healthy, and continuous enterprise. These folks adamantly declared my suggestion was utopian and unachievable. They claimed the survival instinct ingrained in our basic human nature is immovable and requires greed and competition to win at all costs. They believe humanity is wired to compete to the finish, and the world community will never gain enough trust among people to accept a co-creative environment.

I expected such a reply. Of course, they—and I can imagine many politicians, educators, and leaders of industry, and perhaps even you—would say the same with as much emotion as these men and women. Carried throughout history, most of today's businesses, centers for learning, and political agendas achieve results through ego-driven models for success. Driven by the fear of lack, or ultimately, an unconscious fear of death, success is gained by out-thinking, out-maneuvering, and conquering the competition. Winning at all costs and changing laws and rules along the way to accomplish the goal of winning supersedes conscientious decision making.

Competitive achievement taps the primal thrill of the hunt, which is heady and stimulating. Even if the outcome is productive and/or profitable, fear based, ego-driven success earned at the expense of someone or something else, like the destruction of a competing business, misuse of hired labor, depleting an animal species, or polluting the environment, is not sustainable. Under this model, success erodes over time. We are witnessing these effects today, economically, socially, and environmentally.

How can we change this approach to achieving success through soul thinking? Like a weed-choked garden, original ego thinking needs to be dug out by the roots. Business and social models need to be created to achieve safe, successful, and wholesome results in the long run. Soul thinking needs to be transplanted in conscience-rich soil.

The algorithm for soul thinking in making fruitful choices is the same as working out a math problem, or a scientific formula. When there is a stated desire or goal, all available choices to achieve the outcome should be considered. It helps to make a chart and/or create a think tank with everyone involved in the decision-making process.

First, list desired choices with means of achieving them, including expenditures, manpower, resources, materials, financial gains, and most importantly, byproducts and consequences of the outcome.

Then, to each choice of action, comes the task of asking who or what will benefit from this choice? Then, who or what will be harmed? The next step is to continue adding solutions to possible harmful outcomes until no harmful results remain.

Tempering the ego when it comes to financial issues is the greatest challenge. In business for example, the final analysis may satisfy all other needs, and create a satisfactory bottom-line profit—acceptable, but perhaps less profitable than an ego-driven model. So, the moral and financial implications behind that result need to be hammered out to a soulful, sustainable conclusion. Conversely, the final analysis may satisfy all requirements and be enormously profitable. Both results need to be soulfully and conscientiously embraced.

The next questions in business: How much profit is enough? How best to distribute the earned profits?

After personal and business needs are met, and an over-abundance of profit remains, is it plausible to consider philanthropy to continue the momentum of creating?

Employing soul-motivation with logic to address each issue for a successful outcome creates a clear and satisfying approach to a desired goal without backlash. The results: personal satisfaction, community contribution and continued prosperity. The same algorithm applies to personal goals.

Of course, every soulfully made outcome will be different because every desired goal is different. For example, a person seeking to open a school will require different talents and achieve bottom-line results infinitely different from entrepreneurs launching a billion-dollar business. In other words, decisions in every field made from dignity, integrity, and grace, instead of fear and greed, achieve the desired goal to everyone's satisfaction and leaves a clean footprint in its wake.

Now, let's address human development through the millennia and how soul thinking may be the missing key:

Humanity's roots in history currently claim two major origins. The first, Creationism, is the belief God created the world/universe as described in the Bible and man, specifically, in his image. (I raise my hand on this one. I've seen enough to believe this is true.) The second origin, Darwinism, is the belief man evolved as a species, including survival of the fittest. (I honor this theory. There exists so much proof of an evolutionary process on the planet that this cannot be ignored.)

While both views are exceptional, neither Creationism nor Darwinism cites the role of the soul as an integral tool in the human fabric. I want to explore the possibility of how soul thinking, applied to these two prevailing views on man's beginning can drastically change man's future.

Regarding Creationism: What if our ego-driven approach to success is rooted in the biblical story of Adam and Eve? Could it be that competitive achievement began with Adam and Eve accepting the doubts created by their awakened egos and believing they were driven from the Garden of Eden because they fell from God's esteem? If this religious story describing the "fall of man" is taken as truth, then I say, a flaw exists in this thinking. Accepting the fear-based belief of Adam and Eve falling from grace and driven by God from Eden is mistaken, ego-created thought.

Why do I say this? Because from my soul encounter with the Holy Spirit all those years ago, I remain convinced God would never have a negative or punitive reaction to anything he creates, including Adam and

Eve. God is absolute and complete Love. Love only creates perfection. Love does not punish. And, most importantly, love honors Free Will. Meaning, through this gift of unwavering freedom, God cannot protect us from the repercussions of our choices. Indeed, the results may appear as punishment.

From my soul-based insights, I believe Adam and Eve never departed Eden. I suggest our "first parents" became blinded to Eden because they chose to abandon their soul connection to God, or Creation, in favor of accepting the doubts and questions generated by their awakened ego.

I suggest the "Tree of Knowledge" is symbolic for requiring proof instead of living by Trust in God. Perhaps the serpent which enticed Eve to "eat fruit from the tree of knowledge" was the awakening ego, causing a terrifying sense of doubt and fear.

The ego, this new and powerful tool became too overwhelming for Adam and Eve to control. When the ego expressed doubt, fear arose. When fear arose, Trust in God seemed too fragile to accept because, suddenly, so many questions and fears seemed impossible to answer—appearing greater than the simple concept of Trust in God. To me, the loss of Trust in God was the advent of evil.

Next claim in Creationism is that God punished the first couple for eating from the Tree of Knowledge by banishing them from Eden. I suggest that God instructed Adam and Eve not to "eat fruit" from the tree because He understood the repercussions of trusting the ego—and the pain and harm it would cause them. His instructions were to protect them, as you would your child, not to keep something special from them, as the serpent (ego) suggested. When they "ate of the tree" or accepted doubt about their relationship with God, Adam and Eve, through Free Will, cut their connection to God and Creation by trading trust for fear. God did not punish them. Once they accepted the "fruit", or the doubts plaguing them, their egos claimed they deserved punishment, and with all the fears and doubts the ego generated, they believed this conclusion as real.

God simply spoke the truth about how Adam and Eve's new world perspective would change when they used Free Will to abandon their souls for their awakened egos. In abandoning their soul connection, their surrounding world seemed foreign. Their peace lost. This was due to their actions, not God's punishment. And He warned them!

In return, when their world shifted, their awakened egos translated their loss of Eden as punishment—not their conscious choice. God, in his love, could only honor their decision to view the world through the fruits of their actions because, once again, love honors Free Will. Since God, and Eden, are purity and Truth, Adam and Eve could not return—or see Eden— through their doubts and fears.

An analogy I use for Adam and Eve losing Eden would be as if God stood on a shore in Eden and watched them climb onto a ship and sail away. He had to let them go, knowing the suffering they would endure. The remedy? With our awakened souls, we can return to a life of Eden, as God invites us every waking day. His waiting continues—all the way up to now. No punishment, just undying love for us to Believe, Act and be Grateful.

One more time (because this is so very important), as His creations, God honors our Free Will. So, God continues to create, giving us the choice to create alone, through ego-driven thought which will destroy us, or awaken back to Him through our soul connection, and create our world perfectly through Him. Or, in other words, allow Him to manifest through us. Today's jargon is calling this the Law of Attraction. Thoughts Becoming Things. But no one seems to emphasize these positive results can only be completed properly through soul thinking.

Again, when Adam and Eve accepted their insistent and attractive ego, without trusting their soul connection to God, they became dominated by doubt and fear. They consciously stepped away from understanding their sublime soul connection to God in their ability to create—and lost Him. Their perfection and their soul connection to God became obscured by doubt. And understandably so. The ego is a heady enticer, not only mentally, but physically. Ego created doubts, and fears generate adrenaline surges in the body which become addictive. I can guarantee most people are unaware of this adrenaline addiction active within their bodies every day.

Consider the possibility that since the ego first spoke within man's mind, creating the duality of good and evil, we have been deluded about the existence of evil, when in Truth, only good exists.

I believe we, as a species, created evil from fear rising within our own minds. Once separated from the soul connection with Eden, humanity felt alone, naked, and separate. Havoc proceeded in the ensuing generations. Think of the biblical rendition of the first children of Adam and Eve, the brothers, Cain and Able. Cain kills his brother out of jealousy. When questioned as to his brother's whereabouts, he replies, "Am I my brother's keeper?"

The belief in lack initiated man's downfall from the beginning. Why? Because the belief in lack is ego-driven, mistaken thinking. There are solutions to lack, especially in today's modern world. Fear of death has caused competition, hoarding and greed throughout human history.

Think about it. Let's say you are a soul-driven person, celebrating your life and those around you. You have achieved wealth through exciting work, enjoying the fruits of your talents, understanding God continues to create through you. Now, let's say a community or world catastrophe occurs and you have the wherewithal to help overcome the crisis. Don't you believe that you would help—either alone, or by rounding up capable individuals in your sphere of influence? Yes. You know you would. You (and your compadres) would see this moment of aid as a God-gifted opportunity to help. And in helping others, those who've been helped rise to the occasion, doing the same, until the crisis is met. We've seen this heroism performed many times already, in response to environmental calamities and acts of terrorism. While environmental tragedies wreak havoc, human-induced tragedies rend the heart. Acts of terror would never exist if humanity functioned as soul-based individuals.

When the concept of abundance is embraced, we feel honored to know we are our own, each other's and the planet's keepers, simply by being our pure, soulful selves. When man was given dominion over the earth, the gift was a huge responsibility requiring courage, truth, and love—not a mindless rampage over the world to achieve "what we want at all costs" because humans are the highest order. Returning to soul thinking will get us back on track.

Simply stated, our unique talents across every culture are meant to work together to create abundance. The planet is perfectly capable to sustain every one of us once we understand our own purpose on this earth. Using our intellect to ignite our souls and control our egos will achieve perfection in all aspects of our lives.

Now, let's examine the Darwinian approach to human evolution and apply soul thinking to this discussion. Imagine that classic, progressive portrait of man evolving from primate status walking on feet and knuckles to finally standing erect. Our human ancestors are said to have existed for nearly six million years, yet humans supposedly evolved about 200,000 years ago.

History records the Stone Age at 60,000 BC and civilization as we know it began about 6,000 years ago. The Industrial Age began only a tad over 200 years ago! So much has changed for the better throughout the ages, yet so much physical, psychological, and spiritual debris lay in progress's wake. We hear enough in the media to know something is very wrong in the direction humanity is headed.

What was, and continues to be, the greatest downfall throughout all the ages is that fear remains the driving force behind most innovative, intellectual, spiritual, and technological evolution. Man's forward development throughout the ages systematically and consistently viewed the world through ego-based, fear-driven thought, which melded one era into the next by sacrificing lives and cultures of the less powerful to achieve dominance. The motive? You may say power and wealth, but those motives boil down to simply wanting to feel safe. We cannot consider "survival of the fittest" when waging war; mass human destruction has little to do with genetic evolution. Even today, the world's global powers are motivated to garner wealth over human welfare to feel safe, all in the name of progress.

And this is the sadness behind progress throughout man's evolution. Inventing, constructing, finding cures, education and science, financial acquisitions, and so on, conducted through ego-driven thought, creates progress but at a high price to humanity and the planet. Progress has achieved so much but with damaging byproducts. Our eroding well-being is now visible with the slowly fraying state of our planet. Should earth's delicate balance fail, we will be destroyed. Never mind terrorism, political views, greed, cultural inequality, or starvation. Through exploitation or war, if we deplete and destroy planet resources, we won't have a planet to sustain near-future generations, let alone maintain conflicts over diversifying beliefs! Please understand. I am not trying to instill fear. On the contrary, my intention is to instill understanding of the truth, and eliminate fear as a motivational tool.

Fear of death and need for survival brought the original humans from trees and caves to explore their world but fear also supplied clubs and weapons turned on each other to survive. The ages have brought amazing growth and awful destruction. Explicit needs spawned new inventions, beliefs, and cultural development, but sometimes at the expense of fellow men, animals, and the planet. Everything wonderful in man's evolution continues to become tainted with toxic byproducts of fear: pollution, persecution, crime, greed, disease, etc. The more sophisticated humanity becomes with today's thinking, the more danger arises among all the good accomplished.

For example, mounting islands of plastic debris float in the oceans killing wildlife while threatening never to decompose. Plastics, while invented in the late 1800's, didn't become widespread in use until after the second world war in 1945 and again in the 60's and 70's. That's less than 80 years ago. One person's lifetime!

I cannot swim in the beautiful Indian River running along my current hometown due to pollution from sewage and fertilizer run-off, which is infecting the wildlife and natural vegetation living on the river. Pesticides are killing not only us, but pollinators like birds, butterflies and our precious bees needed to keep trees and flowers growing. Genetically modified seeds. Bio-hazardous chemicals. Preservatives in goods and foods. All biproducts of human progress and all potentially harmful.

Why? Once again, because we, as a species, conduct our daily activities from a fear-based, or worse, unconscious world view—achieving results and a financial bottom line without understanding or caring about the ecological and spiritual trauma we create.

Now, let's say the ego, as a fear-motivated, primitive tool for early humans, served its purpose during those formative years as protection against harsh climates, raiding tribes, and dangerous animals. As the centuries progressed and humanity evolved, so did the ego. Only, the ego grew stronger when it should have quieted. The ego, like the soul, is an entity within us wishing to survive. As I said before, the ego does so at the expense of its carrier. When ego thinking floods masses of people, major destruction occurs. Wars, riots, and genocide waged throughout the centuries prove this point.

Ego driven reasoning was most certainly instrumental in encouraging the arrogance that expanded empires by dividing, conquering, and claiming ownership of unwilling dominions through violence and subjugation. We recall these events as history. Yet, empire after empire expired because they were founded on violence and fear. And the same approach continues today, if not physically through war, then economically through commerce. Shall we not learn from history?

If we have evolved according to Darwinism, then I suggest we have arrived at a point in our evolution where living an ego-driven life for survival is no longer in humanity's best interest. Our understanding of technology, economics, and medicine, to name a few, should suffice in removing the terror of death generated by the ego. The fact is: No one gets out of this life alive! Once we understand this truth and make peace with it through our souls, fear dissolves. Our intellect should be showing us that we can and may, if soul driven, use what we know to create abundance for all until we have finished this journey on earth. Ego-driven, fear-based thinking has become a careening vehicle about to take humanity over the precipice. Soul driven thinking will halt the momentum.

Now, let's address Darwin's perspective on all species evolving—including us. The list of extinct species certainly raises a brow, mostly because these plants and animals could not withstand the changing environment. Can you see, as I do, that humanity as a species has evolved enough, and become wise enough, to adjust and grow with our environment in a healthy symbiotic manner? Soul thinking presents the answer to our continued co-existence with the earth and each other. The same applies to the Creationist viewpoint. We, as human beings, can turn hurtful, destructive behavior "off" simply by using Free Will to engage the intellect to control the ego, open the soul, and refuse to accept fear-based thinking. The process and the resulting solutions many times are surprising and rewarding.

Silencing the ego will take effort. Once one is aware of the internal chatter consuming much of our waking time, especially when we are not focused, the ego becomes easy to address, and silence.

Unless an answer to a problem enhances our physical and spiritual world, the choice should be reconsidered over and again, until there is no negative impact. This is soul thinking. This is the approach so many of today's young entrepreneurs and inventors are asking today's leaders to employ. In fact, young thinkers are adopting the logic behind soul thinking into new technology, inventions and solutions, many times unknowing they tap into soul thinking. Our children are soul-evolving and smarter than we are in so many ways.

By investing in Trust in God and instilling a belief that everything works out—because it does—results will be achieved universally and with excitement and success. By eliminating fear in favor of trusting, even when no answer immediately exists, the Earth will take her place as the living, breathing contributor to our species she is, and always has been. Just look at a photo of the planet taken from space. The Earth is a phenomenon.

The time has come to change history for us, for future generations, and for the planet by calming the ego and employing soul thinking to reconnect with Creation. Simply switching gears to soul thinking will initiate solutions to overcome all existing adversities with today's technology, global trade, and community awareness, be it across the street or across the planet.

All this rhetoric may not be new to you. But I didn't truly understand the depths of this thinking until gifted with the insight igniting that "Aha!" moment when the Holy Spirit touched my soul. God's Creation reaches far wider that the limits of this earth's atmosphere. He constantly calls to us every time we open our eyes and take a breath. His unconditional and overwhelming love has shown us, through centuries of spiritual teachers, and moments of awe in observing nature, how to be a part of His Creation.

It is time to listen.

Opening your awareness to see that ego-driven fear propels wrong decisions may be new information to you. If so, I want to say once more: Once we engage the soul to participate in every single decision we make as individuals and a society, this downward spiral plaguing humanity will halt shockingly fast.

The first challenge will be in getting folks to tap into their souls. I suspect people, young and old, living in cities and socially biased climates who have survived using aggression and violence will be our toughest targets to win over. They have been living by instinct and "the sword" for generations, if not always. Given the centuries of history behind humanity functioning from an ego-driven world view, the task seems nearly impossible, especially in getting untrusting minds to grasp the possibility of the peaceful, intangible soul. The ego, which has been accepted and described in so many psychological papers, also is intangible, but for reasons I can only guess, the soul has been ignored.

No longer.

I submit that on an evolutionary level, we have arrived. I believe humanity has evolved enough to know the difference. Fear is no longer necessary as a tool for survival. As a species, soul thinking is our new evolution.

Once soul thinking is employed, fear will dissolve. All aspects of living will make sense. The results? An exciting, abundant, and generous world where each of us, simply by who we are, combine our talents to create meaningful and joy-filled lives, which is why we were born on this jewel of a planet in the first place.

Now, I am not talking any political definition that fosters a "beige" mentality where everyone owns everything equally. In our colorful, soul-driven world, we each achieve our individual success simply by employing our talents for our benefit and the benefit of others. In return, we receive our compensation—financially, emotionally, and spiritually, according to our works and our generosity of spirit.

Think about this, as well. We ask kids, "what do you want to be when you grow up?" Many times, they have an answer. Their answer may change as time progresses, but given a chance, they do have an answer. We as parents, guardians, teachers, friends should do whatever we can to encourage these kindling dreams and see where they lead. Our feelings have no place for consideration when a child declares a personal goal. At that point, all they require is encouragement. Yet in the past, someone "who knows better" may have discouraged a child from moving toward their desired goal because they did not agree or consider the ramifications of discouraging a child.

I know first-hand. Most of my childhood dreams were scrutinized way too closely for me to comfortably consider as future possibilities. What I think ironic, however, is my ego lamented (tortured me, really) for the years of growth it took me to arrive at my desired goals until I learned about and engaged soul thinking. I was able to quiet my ego as I achieved my dreams in an unexpected way, and far greater than I could have imagined. I see now, my journey went exactly as intended because I had to learn to arrive. My wish is to save you, and future generations, from having to wait to reap the rewards of soul thinking.

Here are three steps, using the Ego, Intellect and Soul, I suggest for yourself and anyone in your life, in forming or continuing a soul driven life path.

Employ the Ego: The ego is your talent-discovery tool. If you have not already, take time to learn what excites you. Read books, explore the Internet, join classes, interest groups, or travel to points of interest. Make lists of your talents and strengths. What you do well, what you don't do well. (Both are okay! Love yourself for the individual you are!) Set goals, be they for fun, budget, or business. Do this for yourself often and encourage this curiosity in the children around you. This process gives the ego free reign to discover where talents lay.

Anyone who feels they have no talent, perhaps may have been criticized through life, or felt abandoned to the point where the ego was harmed—leaving a critical and unkind self-worth in its wake. If you relate to this point, I suggest you take a deep breath and remind yourself that you are an intentional creation of unbridled love because God knows exactly how you can continue His Creation. I invite you to take a new look at yourself and see the beauty you perhaps may not have had the courage to share. Look at it this way: Everything you've lived through has been a learning tool. Decide what works and does not work for you— and soulfully choose your direction. Start with small steps, or not!

With today's medical advancements, life can last a very long time. A long life gives us opportunities to change our goals, add to our talents, and share what we do in our communities for our lifetime. All of this is accomplished by tapping into the ego to explore what excites us, then simply act, and be ourselves. No matter what role is chosen. Tapping into the ego to reveal your talents is where you discover who you are and why you were born.

Use your Intellect: The intellect is our research gatherer. The more insights one garners the better able to discern. Get as much of an education as you desire. Encourage everyone in your life to explore every avenue opened to them. The ego harvests your information to make talent choices, especially if "what you want to be" isn't clear for you. "Dead ends" in decision making usually come from insufficient information. Keep learning! Instill an excitement for learning in the children in your life. Learn all you can from individuals you admire. Learning throughout your lifetime for both your intellectual and spiritual growth, eliminates closed-minded thinking, and cements the core foundation of your world view.

Ignite your Soul: Like exercising to strengthen muscles, or eating well to nourish your body, tapping your soul will require a modicum of practice until it comes naturally.

As I mentioned earlier, tapping your soul is simply acknowledging its presence, and trusting its purpose. When you acknowledge your soul it reacts immediately, and you will feel it, usually as a tingle of awareness, or a feeling of relaxation or calm. Initially, you may dismiss the feeling, but here is where employing faith is huge. When you act through your soul, meaning your intention is for your good and the good of others, put your feelers out, you will soon be able to recognize the responses you receive are soul-driven, especially when responses arrive from places you never expected.

Learn to funnel all the talent energy created from your ego and your intellect through your soul. How? Your soul is your unwavering filter for right and wrong. Most times, simply asking through your soul if a decision or choice is right, the answer brings a sense of calm. (Whereas the ego acting as conscience may bring turmoil in decision making.) Soul recognition awakens the proper discernment in your choices of creating power and strength, success, planet awareness, harmony, joy, and most importantly, love.

When in doubt, ask your soul to bring answers. Understand, you may get results in ten minutes, ten days, or ten years, but no matter. By using the fearless, trilateral gifts of ego, intellect, and soul, you will know you are on the right path. And never hesitate to explain the soul's existence to children. You will be surprised how quickly and naturally they tap into soul thinking and make beautiful choices.

Start now. Quiet your mind, even if for a few seconds. In the silence, greet your soul and simply feel. You will sense the calm. From this point of calm and stillness, your ability to create flows strongest. Trust the process.

Your soul is always listening, always waiting to work for you. You will soon learn to recognize answers that arrive from soul-initiated inquiry. Answers seem to arise from a calmer and deeper place. Use your education, your inborn talents, your personality. Then, instill faith in the power of the soul and you will receive all you need.

Anger and irritation arise from ego-based restrictions of thought. Simply use your intellect to examine the source of negative reactions. Once you identify the source of negativity, gently refuse to accept the motive because it no longer serves you in a positive way. This gives the opportunity to recreate a positive response and put the ego at ease. Hardships will take on a new meaning for learning. I see soul-filled results daily and continue to be surprised every time I receive an answer. What a gift!

CHAPTER SIX

The Power of Soul Thinking

When I began to use soul thinking, I used to play a game with God to employ the Law of Attraction. For example, at one point in my family life, we were faced with the decision of whether we should move again. My husband's job in the northeast had taken its course and he was exploring possibilities in Florida. We were living in my dream home. I had no desire to leave. When we bought the hundred-year-old colonial, I believed I would grow old and die in that home. I loved it very much. Yet, for the good of our family, this move seemed like the thing to do.

I clearly remember the Sunday when I initiated soul thinking for an answer. Sitting in my home parish church, I said to God, "If we are supposed to move, give me three signs." So, verbally, I was placing my trust in God's hands. Or, in other words, I trusted my soul to use God's energy to create a clear space to see what filled it, so that my intellect could register my course of action.

As I walked from the church a friend approached. She said, "Kathleen, if you ever decide to sell your home, I know someone who wants to buy it."

I drove away a bit surprised that I heard my first answer within minutes. The following morning, my husband received a call from work saying not to come in. His job was terminated. I looked at the sky and said, "A little drastic, Lord. Don't you think?" And later in the day, I received a cancellation notice in the mail from my home insurance company. Our homeowner's policy would not be renewed. After calls to other insurance companies, I learned none of them were willing to insure us because of new flood zoning. Bam. Within 24 hours, I had my three signs. I realized we were supposed to sell the house.

Was I sad? Yes. Did I now believe moving was the right thing to do? Absolutely. I still miss the house today, but the move opened so many new doors and experiences for me and our family, that there was no mistake in our decision. After all, it was only a house. And your home is where you lay your heart, no?

My point is, when soul thinking is engaged, there is no need for stress. No reason to worry. You can make your soul-generated request, turn off the ego's internal chatter creating worry, and go about your business with a trusting heart. Believing the answer will come takes faith and trust—and a willingness to accept the answers you receive!

Think about it. In any situation you've experienced, hasn't there been a solution? The results may not have been what you expected, but didn't the situation work out in the long run? So why worry? Simply, believe everything will work out, take any steps necessary to move towards your goal, then carry on truthfully and honestly. All will evolve properly.

Okay, so you may say, there's a fun story, but what about serious events in life? Like dealing with a tragic illness, bankruptcy, or an untimely death of a loved one. Some situations appear plainly wrong, many times cruel. And they are. We, who cherish life and our loved ones so completely, cannot wrap our minds around the meaning of tragic events, illness, or death.

In many instances, someone suffering illness can beat the odds by absolutely believing they will survive. My sister did this when battling uterine cancer almost forty years ago. She is alive today because she refused to accept death. With a two-year old and a set of newborn twins at home, she vowed to live for their sakes. (A soul decision for the good of her children.) She defeated her illness when surviving that cancer seemed impossible. How? She refused any negative thoughts or reactions from herself or others. Fearlessly, she chose life, underwent the therapy she needed to heal, and did.

But sudden death? With the greatest love for anyone who lived through this pain, I humbly offer that tapping into the soul for guidance, using trust and faith to overcome the anger and void left in death's shadow will slowly renew one's strength and willingness to carry on. Life and Death are the Alpha and Omega of human existence. Death is why our journey through life is so very precious. Perhaps, *accepting* the pain of loss, instead of *resisting* the pain of loss, may encourage the surviving souls to heal and maybe even help others who experience the same tragedy.

I am thinking about a neighbor who lost her twenty-year-old son in the travesty of 9/11 in Manhattan. Many of us know people who lost loved ones in that act of terrorism. In many cases, sudden loss of a loved one is due to the actions of others by accidents, medical malpractice, murder, terrorism, the list goes on.

It is important to understand that the inability to forgive, forget, and/or carry on comes from the ego. The ego twists the violent or negligent acts of others as pointed cruelty against the person who died and their survivors. The ego hammers the pain repeatedly in the imagination, making the survivors suffer more than any one person can stand. (And usually when the tragedy is public, the media fosters such pain with continuous and horrific news reports.)

Understanding we are all connected through our souls, even after death, opens the possibility that those souls who departed know the agony permeating the lives of their survivors. Believing that our soul connection to others transcends the physical body can allow the departed souls to soothe the aching, surviving souls. They will if we let them.

In moments like these, if we do not engage the soul to seek understanding, the ego will have a field day with the trauma of loss and refuse to let a person heal. Life will go on. We can carry on with unwavering faith in our soul's connection with that which we cannot see, or let the ego control our emotions and keep the pain alive which ruins the remainder of many lives.

In the name of the departed, I suggest the least we can do is continue to create goodness for our own good and the good of others. The choice to depend on soul thinking when tragedy strikes will help ensure that tragedies occur less and less in the future, especially with tragedies based on crime. Why? Crime arises from fear. When soul thinking becomes the norm, there will be no more fear. Hence, no need for crime. There will be no more criminals. Yes. This unbelievable scenario can become our reality.

Another personal example is that I, and most of my family, were with my father, Herby, when he died from cancer in 1989. He died at the age of 61. While I recognized the honor of being with him when he passed, his passing was my first encounter with death, face-to-face. I watched my father—my hero—take his last breath. I was so aware of the moment his soul moved on. I looked around the room for his spirit.

Moments later, my ego kicked in at the horror of realizing Dad's body was lifeless and he was gone. I would never see him again, hear his voice, listen to him tell jokes or play his banjo. There would be no more days on the boat with him or coming to visit him and Mom. I believed no one could ever understand the void and the pain ripping through my body. Trying to escape the horror, I jumped into my car and sped away, unable to catch my breath while blindly driving down the empty road.

It wasn't until I heard a soft voice inside my head saying, "Stop her. She's screaming," that I realized I was howling through my tears. I pulled the car over and closed my eyes. I begged God for understanding.

I asked my soul to open and fill me with the calm I needed. My soul responded. My breath returned to normal. I cried more deeply, and my sorrow began to sooth the ache in my entire body. My tears were cementing me in the moment. My soul acknowledged my pain and made it okay for me to feel the devasting loss. I still lived. I had the responsibility to join my family in burying my father's body, no matter how hard the task. My Dad's soul was somewhere out there, and I decided I would continue to stay in contact with him through my soul. I also knew, with time, I would find joy again and live to honor my father's life as I knew him.

In the thirty-something years since Dad departed, I have felt his presence many times. I experienced life-like dreams with him (as have my siblings) and knew they were real. In times of stress, I have heard Dad playing the banjo in those quiet moments before waking. I awakened, fully knowing he was playing for me to give me strength to deal with the issues at hand. And recently in a dream, my father called me on the telephone. For the first time in over thirty years, I heard him speak, as clear as day. The joy in his voice thrilled me. I texted all my siblings as soon as I awoke and shared his visit. Herby was the type of man who would make every effort to keep in touch with his family, even after life on earth. And, he has.

Results such as these come from soul thinking. One may interpret these experiences as a manifestation of one's imagination, but I offer that a willingness to suspend a need for factual evidence gives our souls a chance to communicate with us cognitively. We simply must trust, or have faith, that this fact is true.

When we engage our souls in our day-to-day lives, those who love us, whether alive or passed on, continue to support us in ways far greater than we can imagine. You must be open to the power of your soul, and the souls of loved ones. Have faith in yourself and trust our souls' good works. You will see the fruits and feel the resulting power.

Now, when you begin recognizing responses from your soul, it is important to understand soul communication is a natural phenomenon. The newness of the experience may excite you. That is terrific! It's fun to share your experiences with others. Sharing is a wonderful way to reinforce the power at work between your soul and Creation.

However, be aware. The ego may act. Be cautious of letting yourself believe you have special powers because you now recognize this spiritual connection, or you are unique because of these experiences. I'm sure as you read this you recognize the pitfall one can create by adopting this egoist thinking. Believing this connection makes you stronger or better than others will separate you from others once more, when in fact, by remaining in soul thinking you will feel more strongly connected to others, the world you see, and cannot see.

So again, I repeat, while the soul has been acknowledged throughout the ages, few people understand the soul as a gift for use now, while we live in today's world. Our soul is the single most powerful tool we possess to accomplish our personal goals with wisdom, love, and accuracy, especially when used in conjunction with our ego and intellect. The only way to create this perfect, unilateral triangle of existence is to obliterate fear. Read on!

CHAPTER SEVEN

Obliterating Fear

I invite you to obliterate fear from your life. How? Employing what I call The Three A's.

- Acknowledge
- Ask
- Act

Here is the process:

First, when fear arises, don't resist. *Acknowledge* it. Look fear right in the eye and say, "Okay, so I'm afraid." And please remember, if the reaction is not fear, but anger, hate, jealousy, self-doubt, or envy (to name a few negative emotions) you can apply this same direct approach to explore those negative reactions because all negativity comes from fear.

Second, *Ask* yourself why this challenge is frightening. Have I been challenged to achieve something I've desired, but the action is outside my comfort zone? Have I contracted a serious illness and I am afraid of dying? Do I feel animosity for this person whom I am supposed to love because I am jealous, or feel neglected? Am I confronted with a dangerous person or situation?

If the situation is life-threatening and you don't have the time to explore your emotions, immediately surrender your fear to Trust, physically exhaling as you do. You will feel the calmness you need rise inside you to get through the situation. Then proceed in the best manner to ensure your safety.

In the past, I found that in moments of anxiety or even terror, surrendering to Trust was all I could do! In hindsight, I was always amazed at how I either solved the issue myself or I received immediate aid. In every instance, I was left thinking, I have amazing angels. Tapping into soul energy can create minor miracles in times of crisis. (Oh, and I do have amazing angels because angels are soul-based and do assist us, but this, too, is another matter of trust.)

So, when confronting fear, it does not matter whether one acts reflexively, or has the luxury of time to decide the required action. By simply acknowledging fear, you immediately become centered in the moment. This acknowledgement ignites your soul awareness. What I am saying, is you do not have to consciously think, "Ok, time to tap into my soul." No. Learning to be aware of fear when it surfaces in your mind and body is all you need do. You will feel calmness arise within you, or merge with the adrenaline surge needed for immediate and necessary reaction. In all cases, the removal of fear gives you more clarity to achieve the necessary, positive results.

Which leads to step three: Despite fear, *Act* anyway! If research is required to get an answer, take the time to do the research. If a decision needs to be reached and you truly are unsure of which decision to make, try "putting the question out there" and await the results. (Such as my game of asking God to give me three signs as proof I should sell my house.) But be clear. Your question must be concise. Then, be certain you will receive answers by creating a clear, open space through the soul. By this I mean, have no expectations on answers. Act as if you simply opened the door to a sunlit room or opened the gate to an open field where you watch to see who, or what, arrives. And many times, the answers come from such an unlikely source, that you know the response is specific to your request.

When you Trust, and ask through your soul, the answers come. Every time. But remember, you must be willing to do the work to achieve the outcome once you have your answers! Soul thinking is not waving a magic wand. Soul thinking is tapping into your God-source to aid your chosen actions through life's adventures, be they exciting good times, character and career growth, or challenging moments.

Here's the irony in ego-based thinking. Many of us do not realize that when experiencing fear, past learned, negative behaviors trigger into action. Past learned behaviors engage ego-thinking. Since ego thinking is always fear based, the choices made will come from a place of past fear, and therefore not serve well.

Ego thinking immediately separates us from the soul's connection to our true source of Power. Why? Because fear replaces trust with mistrust in ourselves. Mistrust diminishes our effective personal power. Why? Because ego thinking always creates inner conflict by magnifying negative or positive possibilities that may or may not exist. Past learned behaviors born from fear may cause one to misjudge or mistrust what is happening, when in fact, the soul has perceived correctly. Fear keeps one from acting correctly, i.e., with anger instead of compassion; competitively instead of constructively; erratically instead of logically.

Also, remember that besides causing damage emotionally and logically, fear-based energy becomes negatively charged, which physically floods the body with corrupting, chemical chain reactions which not only harm the cells and organs of the body, but confuse thought processes. Decisions made from fear seldom yield positive results. Hence, stress, conflict, regrets, poor business decisions, or prolonged illness follow suit. And, it has been proven that stress causes premature aging. Who needs accelerated aging?

I said this earlier and know this sounds goofy but think of your favorite superhero. What is so attractive about him or her? My superhero is Superman. Superman not only acknowledged his superpowers and knew how to use them, but he was unwavering in understanding the value he brought to others when using his powers for good. Meanwhile, he remained humble and did everything he could to blend in with the world around him.

Now, superheroes may have their angry moments, as do we all. What makes our superheroes great is that even when angry, or with danger barreling down on them, they recognize the emotion, grow calm, and act. Their attitude is not to obliterate their opponent as much as to stop the danger. Unfortunately, many times stopping the danger obliterates the opponent. (Ego-driven, fear-based actions tend to result in destruction.)

Only, superheroes don't gloat over the tragedy. They simply get the job done.

The same is true with soul thinking. When a perceived "danger" arises, be it physical, intellectual, or spiritual, surrendering to the calm that immediately arises from tapping into the soul produces results more powerful than any ego generated, fear-based response. Why? Because the results will bear fruit, or get the job done, as intended.

Here's the most exciting point to initiating soul thinking: Removing the fear response is simply a matter of changing your mind. When you understand that ego creates fear, and reinforces fear through past learned behaviors, those behaviors will no longer have an appeal. Forming new thought patterns brings new emotional, intellectual, and spiritual freedom. In return, trusting soul thinking as a power source becomes easier. The new results achieved from soul thinking act as proof, should proof be required. True power, however, is found when engaging faith. Faith is believing God literally works through you, fearlessly. It is that simple. Feel free to change your mind to claim this truth. The responsibility is yours. No one can change your mind for you.

A quote from, *A Course in Miracles*, by Helen Schucman sums up this understanding of faith over fear beautifully:

"Everything you have taught yourself has made your power more and more obscure to you. . . Be willing then, for all of it to be undone, and be glad that you are not bound to it forever."

How to change your thinking becomes clearer when you understand the cause and effect of your thoughts. Your mind, or more pointedly, your ego, is chattering all the time. While showering, getting dressed, grocery shopping, commuting to work, sitting in meetings, cooking, visiting with friends, etc., if you are not concentrating completely on the moment at hand, your mind is wandering. Or, more succinctly, your ego is chattering.

Wandering thoughts not only eject you from the "now" of the moment, but they usually are unkind to you, or about something you did, or someone/something you are observing, creating worry or criticism. Pay attention to where your thoughts wander. There is no reason to respond critically of yourself when you become aware of negative thoughts plaguing your inner mind. Most of the world has become comfortable with this inner dialogue. Hence, ego chatter drives the state of today's thinking. Where there is little soul thinking, there is little generosity of thought.

The more effort taken by the intellect to acknowledge the chatter, like elevator music in the background of our minds, the more gently you can bring yourself back into the moment. Concentrating fully on what you are doing will always silence the chatter. With repeated, conscious vigilance, inner dialogue will eventually cease, and will only commence again when permitted. By the time you master soul thinking over ego thinking, you will also be able to dismiss the negative responses your "other-self" drops into the discussion.

Have you noticed when your ego injects a negative thought, it does not pass through your mind once? Nay! Nay! The ego isn't satisfied with one negative statement. Like a spoiled child, or an unkind guardian, the thought repeats itself, again and again, until you physically react to the pain. Why? Because ego chatter creates a living energy within the body. The repeated negative thought ignites anger, anxiety, or depression, which floods the body with stressful electrochemical reactions. To shake off the physical discomfort, logic engenders negative responses towards someone or something, self-criticism, acting in the wrong direction due to poor motivation, or despair over a situation.

What's worse? The results from ego-driven dialogue do not serve properly. Then, the ego has new fuel to criticize once more, creating a nasty, continuous cycle of negativity. In his book on spiritual awakening, *The Power of Now,* Eckhart Tolle recognizes this painful and negative energy within us as the pain body. The pain body is a collection of negative emotions accumulated in the body throughout our lifetime. This physicality takes on a life of its own and needs to be nourished by creating painful, angry, and self-deprecating thoughts that emotionally torture us. Once released and refueled by our anguish, the pain body goes dormant again, until triggered by another incident that taps an unconsciously stored and painful memory.

The solution? Guard your thoughts. It is now time to use the intellect to retrain the ego to act as intended, instead of running wild. When you feel the onslaught of negative thoughts beginning to spin in your mind, become aware the pain body is coming alive, once more. Do not chastise yourself! Simply observe. Listen to what is being said in your head. Then consider:

- Is the critical thought true, and if it is true, what purpose is served in generating unkind or unproductive thought? Could this thought be better served by using the soul to consider there is a need to be met here, instead of a break-down?

- Is there a valid reason to view another person, situation, or yourself, critically? Or is the criticism permitting the ego to bash you, the situation, and/or others to create an emotional adrenaline rush on which the pain body has come to depend to feel alive and important?

- If there is a constructive assertion to make, would it be better received couched in wisdom and clarity instead of criticism? The former gets the point across with respect, while the latter, again, feeds the critic's ego as the smarter person.

- Would it be more constructive to address the thought with a solution instead of a retribution? This creates a win-win in every way.

- Is the criticism a topic requiring immediate action? Or is the ego/pain body dredging up unnecessary past pain, or a future potential problem? Either scenario keeps a mind pre-occupied with negativity and unable to experience the present moment, when in truth, only the present moment exists. The past is gone. The future is yet to come. So, stay grounded in the moment.

- When the mind dwells on a criticism or stressful topic, ask if this is your belief or one you have been taught. Many times, our core beliefs are adopted through childhood teachings, personal associations and experiences which cause internal struggle because our souls cannot recognize them as Truth. The soul excels at discernment. When the choice is made to reestablish new core beliefs, complete trust in the soul for discernment is required. When newly formed core beliefs excite you, rest assured you are rebuilding in the right direction.

What saddens me most, is that internal criticism arises either to make yourself feel better at the expense of whomever or whatever the internal chatter is attacking, or to make yourself feel awful for actions taken. Either way, unhealthy ego chatter damages mind, body, and spirit. This behavior of the pain body is contrary to why we are present here on earth. I am sure you can see this!

Decisions to remain peaceful threaten the ego's existence. If the ego and pain body cannot feed on your emotional pain, they cannot thrive. Using the intellect to accept the soul as a tool for discernment brings internal peace and awakens awareness to the complete reversal of what many today believe as fact: that we are born separate and alone in this world. In truth, and I repeat, each of us is a necessary thread in the tapestry of existence and are connected soulfully to each other, the planet and Creation. How cool is that?

Once your mind adopts the pattern of analyzing ego chatter, you automatically begin to find a kinder thought or a constructive solution to replace the negative one. Even if the situation at hand is challenging, or difficult because someone else responds negatively, you no longer need to be defensive. You simply need to understand the situation through the soul (i.e., with compassion and curiosity) and be crystal clear with the truth.

When dealing with others, here is where carefully chosen word track communicates your thoughts and intentions clearly. Repeating others' words in your own words with dignity, integrity, and grace, so they know you understand them, helps clarify your response so everyone is understood. This type of soulful "mirroring" conversation creates a safe place for dialogue and to achieve solutions. Understanding yourself and helping others understand you begins the process of dissolving the pain body and re-training the ego to return to its proper job: recognizing the finer qualities of any given situation, person, or yourself. By doing this, you circumvent negative drama to get the job done.

Employing compassion with logic creates wisdom. Wisdom silences ego chatter and gives you a sense of strength through your goodness. Your goodness and strength permeate the space and people around you with palpable energy. As a result, the people around you are inspired to tap their souls (many times, unconsciously) to feel the goodness and strength of their own wisdom.

You will be surprised at the conversations, motivations and actions that arise with the freedom of heart and imagination from soul thinking. What could be more beautiful?

CHAPTER EIGHT

Love Vs. Chaos

I mentioned my father, Herby, already in this work. He wasn't a religious man, yet, he had complete faith in God as a greater power instrumental in his life. When I returned home after my spiritual encounter with the magnificent eye in the triangle, I asked Dad if he'd listen to what I'd witnessed.

"It's weird," I said.

He relaxed in his chair. "Okay. What happened?"

As I mentioned in the beginning of this work, of all the folks with whom I shared my story, I'll never forget how matter-of-fact Dad's reaction was. We were sitting at the round, antique oak table in our kitchen. I described the eye in the triangle, how I felt, and what I saw through the eye. I realized later that Herby chose to listen to me with his soul, instead of his ego. The results? He helped reinforce my experience. He took his money clip from his pocket and pulled out a one-dollar bill. Turning the bill over, he said, "Did it look like this?"

The Great Seal on the back of the U.S. dollar bill holds the unfinished thirteen-stepped pyramid topped off by an eye in a triangle. He said, "If this is what you saw, it can't be bad. Don't worry. You'll figure it out."

It took a while, but I did. These next thoughts are my observations, especially in today's chaotic world, and how they apply to everything I discovered all those years ago.

In my opinion, much of today's aggressive world behavior openly opposes soul-based thinking. Ego-driven needs for power, prestige, profit, etc., dismiss the soul-based approach to those needs as impossible, implausible, or ineffective. Perhaps even threatening. In truth, achieving goals through soul thinking creates power, prestige, and profit for everyone, beginning at individual levels because each of our talents vary. As humans in touch and creating soulfully, we will celebrate each other's accomplishments, no matter how great or small. The take-away from my encounter, which trusts soul living as something wonderful, abundant, enlightening, satisfying and loving, is a concept I think our country—and the world—needs to reconsider. Especially now, when everywhere I look, God is being removed from our lives.

The Being I encountered appeared as an eye in a triangle, which leaves me fascinated and grateful our founding fathers believed enough in God as a higher power to include this symbol on the Great Seal of America printed on our country's currency. (And I wonder: Who else saw this Being to draw the image in the first place?)

This symbol does not delineate a religion, but an essence of spirit, power, and soul. Early cultures, native Americans, and "undeveloped" civilizations that lived, and continue to live, close to the earth understood and respected a power greater than they, active in their universe. It seems the more we advance in technology, the more unnecessarily distant we grow from our true Source.

Trust in God has eroded to the point where reference to God and/or religion of any denomination is being touted as a possible insult to someone else, and therefore, cannot be tolerated. For this reason, mention of God is actively being removed as biased from schools, businesses, and media, to mention a few. I disagree with this action because I witnessed the reality of God as an all-loving Being worthy of recognition, gratitude, awe, and praise. Yet, I will not force my knowledge on anyone although I am eager to share what I have learned.

What I find amusing is that if reference to God is removed from public awareness, the removal will not obliterate God. God exists whether we believe or not. I simply do not understand why anyone finds the mention of our Creator offensive, at all. Unless the thought of God incites fear or anger. And if this is the case, why? The Ego: Easing God Out. Centuries of ego-dominated behavior where the over-active ego works alone, or in masses of like-minded, to annihilate any threatening being, dogma or action to remain alive and safe. Think about it: that destructive drive could systematically eradicate humanity until only a pocket-full of people prevailed who would then mistrust and turn on each other until one surviving being remained. The strongest. Then what? Clearly, such destructive action defies God's Creation—the act and flow of creating. How exhausting to be otherwise.

The bottom line here is that Creation will continue whether humanity does or does not. I cannot believe we exist as a part of Creation to destroy ourselves because we cannot control our egos. Wouldn't it be wonderful to join in Creation instead of ruining our gift to create soulfully?

Once more, please consider the possibility that ego-driven thinking is running amuck politically, economically, and socially. Like a fissure in a dam, the wall of diversity and love on which most of us rely, is in danger of splitting wide open. We, and our children, are being shown that if someone does not think, look, or act like us, he/she is dangerous to our happiness and well-being. And most recently, under the guise of "freedom of choice" children are being taught not to trust who they were born to be, either physically or intellectually. This is chaos.

The current mindset of "demands" for personal and social rights does not maintain the conscious awareness of right and wrong. Current demands are declaring, "I am right, and you are wrong." Or worse, create confusion in an individual's mind which causes internal chaos that continues to feed the ego and the pain body. In chaos, there is no love, no peace, only emotional and/or physical strife which induces stress, distrust, and unhappiness.

What is the difference between the confusing, censoring, and psychologically damaging movements currently flooding our culture and the past actions throughout history of, say, Genghis Kahn and the

Mongol invasions, the Crusades, the sprawling Roman Empire, the first settlers of America against the native inhabitants? Slavery? Or Hitler's actions in the Holocaust? I say, no difference. There can be as much violence found in words and laws as there is in physical assault. And do these destructive actions follow us through the generations? Yes. Why? Because egoic-driven aggression has traveled down the centuries, and to-date, continues.

The good news? We can change this momentum by simply changing our minds.

The Miriam-Webster dictionary defines Free Will as *the freedom of humans to make choices that are not determined by prior causes or by divine intervention.*

The Holy Spirit made it clear that love honors Free Will in all people—which makes us, not God, completely responsible for our actions. Unless we are aware that Free Will is the credo of our soul connection to God, most folks won't even know they can choose. Instead, they will be pigeon-holed into believing fear-driven rules to ensure a sense of safety that ultimately serves a few.

Free Will gives us the freedom to object to someone else's choices, and keep our own choice, with dignity, integrity, and grace. This is diversity, the tapestry of life into which we are all woven, and why we are here today. In diversity, there is nothing to fear when love is honored.

That said, when viewing others or a situation of diversity through the eyes of the soul, a healthy inquiry evolves where love, curiosity, and respect are brought to play when encountering people of other cultures, skin color, intellectual levels, and languages. The desire to know fuels constructive dialogue. A give-and-take of information.

Bottom line? Prosperity. This is Love. It invites curiosity, creativity, conversation, productivity, contentment. Chaos causes anxiety, unhealthy competition, censorship, stifles creativity, pollutes, and most effectively, engenders fear. Chaos makes life, and our emotional constitutions, unbearable.

I respect common courtesy, but I feel social and political courtesies have been abused. Political correctness in today's form is a perfect example of instilling chaos. Someone will always be angry, cast blame, and demand recognition, which means someone is driven by fear—and sets themselves apart from others. A soul connection to God and our fellow man for general health, wealth, and well-being, would not permit the abuse of political correctness. Heck, there would never be a need for political correctness. Courtesy would happen organically.

I choose to respect Free Will and honor other people's opinions, as I believe they will honor mine. I wrote this book to share what I experienced with every soul willing to listen. My hope is that my readers' souls listen—and ignite.

Balancing our three spiritual organs of soul, intellect, and ego, will bring everyone's talents forward for everyone's mutual good. America's founding fathers, as did the founders of so many older countries, despite their active egos, planted their roots using God as nourishment for building their countries and their lives. Understanding our souls exist as conduits to God, for the continuance of his Creation through us, will make everyone and everything richer on this earth. That is Creation. We're here to participate with love, curiosity, and excitement. At the end of the day, the joy of it all will prove, without a doubt, the impossible can happen.

CHAPTER NINE

I Had a Dream

Now, we have reached a point where I want to share how a dream finally obliterated my fear of telling my story. We all know dreams act as tools for the unconscious mind, and are chock-full of symbolism, which like poetry, invite us to unravel their underlying meaning. This dream, and its symbolisms, left me feeling not only liberated, but clear-minded about my intentions for writing this work. So, please, indulge me one last time.

In my dream, I stood on the edge of a high desert butte. The spectacular view left me in awe. The desert below sprawled for miles. Majestic buttes rose in the distance, much like the one on which I stood. The intense colors of azure and gold reflected the sky. Terra-cotta hues painted the desert floor.

As I was absorbing the scene before me, getting comfortable with the dizzying height and the awesome vista, a presence behind my right shoulder said one word, "Jump."

Shocked, I replied, "No! Are you crazy? I'll die."

The voice gently replied, "No, you won't. Jump. As you fall, pump your arms and legs as if you are running. When you hit the ground, you will move forward. You will be fine."

Again, I said, "No. I can't. I won't." My body tensed with fear. Jumping was sheer insanity, instant death. I refused to budge.

The voice said, "Trust me."

Something calmed inside me. I didn't understand how I could possibly jump and survive, but I chose to trust. I jumped. Immediately, my stomach lurched. My breath escaped in a rush. A knot choked my throat. I panicked. Then, I remembered my instructions. I pumped my arms and legs with every ounce of strength as the air blew past me. I felt like an Olympic runner. The ground came towards me, and to my surprise, because I was in motion, instead of crashing, my tiptoe dug into the sand and I bolted across the desert, like I had rockets on my heels. A plume of dust rose behind me like the Road Runner from the Looney-Tunes cartoon. (Got to love dreams!)

After traversing halfway across the desert, I stopped to catch my breath. I looked back. My footprints measured the distance between me and that towering butte. Not only did I jump, not only did I survive, but I ran faster and stronger than I ever had in my life. My heart pounded with excitement. I started jumping up and down, fists in the air like Rocky Balboa in the movie, Rocky, standing on the steps of Philadelphia City Hall. I did it! And not even a scratch. The exhilaration was overwhelming.

In my dream, I returned home to my family. Circled around the table in my parents' kitchen, I announced what I had done, fully expecting them to cheer me on. Instead, they became outraged. They said, "How could you have been so stupid?" "Would you tell your sons to jump off a cliff?" "That was irresponsible and reckless." "What were you thinking?"

I was stunned. My family is supposed to love and support me. Theirs were valid questions, but they missed the point that I had emerged victoriously from the dangerous experience—an experience intended only for me. I walked away, thinking, "They don't get it. They don't understand me."

I awakened and realized this "jump" for me was my soul showing me how, by having trust and faith, I will accomplish more than I can imagine. Taking a leap of faith (trusting my soul thinking) when I make decisions, especially when situations seem impossible, will bring surprising results. Not everyone will understand, but eventually, they will. And, if they do not, it has no bearing on who I am, or why I make the choices intended for me. It does not matter what anyone thinks, when I know from my soul, my decisions are correct.

If by some chance, my initial decision is incorrect, you can be sure that not only will there be a life lesson in the error, but the error will correct itself, exactly when it should. In the long run, when we do what is right, it turns out to be right for everyone else, whether they believe the fact, or not.

Now, DO NOT JUMP OFF A CLIFF! I am not suggesting that you jump or do anything to physically harm yourself. Dreaming I jumped from the cliff was not literally "jumping off" a cliff. The "jump" served as emotional symbolism for me to overcome the hurdles of fearful choices created by the ego in favor of accepting soul thinking for results.

Note, too, that soul thinking is not passive work. In the dream, I had to use my body and my mind, while trusting my soul (the quiet presence behind me), to launch the motion to keep me safe through the fall and achieve my triumph. Before jumping, I imagined if I jumped, I would impact the ground in a mass of broken bones. Hence, my terror, and the same terror anyone one else in their right mind would feel. Until I "jumped", I didn't realize that running in air (pulling from the ether/universe while suspended in "space") would take me farther than I could have possibly imagined once I touched the ground. The entire symbolic dream created the truth of reality for me: Trust in my connection with that which I cannot see and accept the fruits of my trust despite those who may not understand or criticize.

My fear evaporated. The dream cemented my refusal to accept irrational fear any longer in my life, which is why I write this book for you today. Humanity has been governed by laws that created chaos when we exist to conduct our lives through laws of love.

I suggest we examine life's current formula as applied to today's business, communications, politics, education, farming, technology . . . everything we do! Tweaking our human condition so everyone benefits, including the earth, is possible. And please understand, this notion is not a political stance. Perfection is our inheritance. All we must do is:

- Accept the gift of our soul.
- Trust in God.
- Add soul thinking to our intelligence and talents.
- Honor Free will in everyone.

Soul, intellect, and ego, when blended, create a triangle of perfection within us. There is no situation or event in existence that cannot be resolved when soul, intellect and ego are used together in equal parts.

To live a soul-filled life is embracing a world of joy, creativity, and abundance. Like the amazing Being I encountered who had not one iota of negativity to His existence, our world should lovingly and confidently refuse to accept violence, hate, suppression and greed. (By greed, I am not addressing personal financial success from talent-driven achievement. Greed is the fear-based accumulation of wealth at the expense of others, without regard to the negative ripple-effect from the wish to survive, no matter what the cost.)

Soul thinking incorporated into politics, business and religion is the new challenge for today's politicians, educators, leaders of industry and religious leaders. I believe once adopted as a tool for results, soul thinking will change the course of humanity on all levels towards a world most people believe as impossible.

Like TED Talks, I would love to create a forum of today's movers-and-shakers from all walks of life to discuss the change required in humanity's direction by adding soul thinking to the think tank. OMG! I want to be there for those discussions! I am not smart enough to do this alone. My purpose for writing this book is to reach out to each one of you and introduce soul thinking—from the grassroots to the highest echelon of industry, education, science and medicine, business, and technology. I want to work with those who grasp our soul connection to our Creation to bring about humanity's new evolution to joyful, abundant, and fearless living.

We have nothing to lose, and everything to gain. I am dedicated to do my share in this process. If ego driven, I am only one. If soul based, I am connected to the entire planet. That makes me, and you, extremely powerful. With this power, we must accept the responsibility and be ruled by Love: Our source. Our inheritance. Our strength.

Let's get started. The choice is so very simple. Here's how:

1. When you start your day, acknowledge your soul, and invite it to work through you.

2. Be conscious that every person you know, meet, or pass, carries the same need for love as you.

3. Know by simply being you, you have something to teach others.

4. Recognize the gifts others bring, be they great or small, and be willing to use and share what you learn.

5. Understand each day is another opportunity to express your talents and have them gratefully received by others.

6. Greet everyone you meet through the eyes of your soul. I promise. You'll see more than you ever expected.

Thank you, from the depths of my heart and soul, for taking the time to read this work. I hope your soul heard mine. If you have any questions or comments, reach me through my email, SOSkathleenann@gmail.com. I would enjoy hearing from you!

Much love,
Kathleen Ann

Printed in the United States
by Baker & Taylor Publisher Services